Become

a vessel unto honor

Saffie True Kamara

Trilogy Christian Publishers

A Wholly Owned Subsidary of Trinity Broadcasting Network

2442 Michelle Drive

Tustin, CA 92780

For information, address Trilogy Christian Publishing

Rights Department, 2442 Michelle Drive, Tustin, Ca 92780.

Trilogy Christian Publishing/ TBN and colophon are trademarks of Trinity Broadcasting Network.

For information about special discounts for bulk purchases, please contact Trilogy Christian Publishing.

Manufactured in the United States of America

10 9 8 7 6 5 4 3 2 1

Library of Congress Cataloging-in-Publication Data is available.

B-ISBN#: 978-1-64088-965-1

E-ISBN#: 978-1-64088-966-8

Dedication

This book is dedicated to God the Father, Son and, Holy Spirit.
Then to my parents, Ishmael and Kadiatu Bah, my lovely sons Nehemiah
and Noah, and to every woman still searching for her purpose.

Acknowledgments

I want to thank the following:

Thanks to America, the greatest country in the world. What a great country! I am thankful I can serve Jesus freely.

Pastor Thomas George and Pastor Komba Musa, for being my Spiritual Fathers and for demonstrating the love of Christ.

My aunt, Tity Conteh, for all your prayers and being the first person to take me to church when I was a little girl. You are the example of the woman of virtue I want to be one day.

Rachael Fatmata Bangura and Isatu Nabie, for taking care of me, God bless you both for all you did for me.

Isatu Tity Bah Kamara, for your love and continuous support. Every girl needs a sister like you.

My ex-husband, for being there when I needed you the most.

All my sister-friends, for ALWAYS being a shoulder to cry and lean on.

The pastors, elders, and members of Jesus Christ is the Son of God Ministries, my home church for your prayers, love, and support.

The leaders and members of MorningCrew International Christian Fellowship, Women of Prayer, Josiah Generation Youths, and Awakening Fellowship Ministry for your prayers and support in my walk with Christ.

Table of contents

Introduction

Thank you for picking up this book. May it be an inspiration to you as you read it. May it give you a sense of hope and encouragement. Despite your past, family, or cultural background you can rise and become what God has called you to be. Know there's not a life too messed up or too dirty that God cannot clean up and purify for His glory. All we must do is open our hearts and allow Him to come in and help guide and direct us to our calling. Know you do not need to be perfect to be called by God. Do not be ashamed of your past, but willing to be authentic and vulnerable in sharing your story. Authenticity and vulnerability are not signs of weakness, but of strength.

So, I guess this is it, huh? I cannot keep running from the truth. I must listen and stop being selfish because it is not about me. I must obey the word of the Most High GOD. LORD, here I am now, writing, listening to You. Here You have it, I am writing. What I am writing I don't know, but the interesting thing is that You know, and all You want me to do is listen to Your voice.

My name is Saffie, a girl from Sierra Leone, West Africa. For most of my childhood, I had never heard of America a day in my life. But one day it all changed. I think it was some sort of a holiday, I can't really recall what was going on. But what I do remember is that we were sitting on our front porch on Melon street in Wellington, and a call came in for my Dad. He answered, and it was his friend, who was more like a brother to him. They were talking about us winning the DV lottery (a.k.a. green card lottery) and that we needed to go in for an interview for a visa to go to America—the land of opportunities, land of the free, the blessed land. At this point, my father was very happy about the news but at the same time not sure of it all. So, he started asking others for advice and people told him my sister and I were too young to be out of his sight, "And they will be staying with who again? Who do you have in America that's going to receive

1

them?" At the moment, there was no one.

However, my Dad took that leap of faith and went for it anyway. He bought us plane tickets and off we went to Abidjan for the interview. Two weeks later we were granted our visas to enter the United States of America. At this point in our lives, we were not yet saved. I didn't know God for myself and had never asked Him for anything because I did not know who He was. I had heard about Jesus was when my aunty would take us to church with her from time to time. But the only things I liked about church were the praise and worship songs and the candy they gave us to keep us awake for all-night prayers.

But God had a plan for my life that I knew nothing about. Just like when Jeremiah the Prophet was called by God to be a prophet to Judah, "Before I formed you in the womb, I knew you; before you were born I sanctified you; I ordained you a prophet to the nations" (Jeremiah 1:5 NKJV). The LORD knew him before he was formed in his mother's womb, set him apart, and appointed him as a prophet to nations. Very often, we are afraid of what God has called us to be, but what we do not realize is we were born to do that very thing He is calling us to walk in. Jeremiah 1:5 was the call to leadership for the not-so-confident Jeremiah, and we see here how God is telling him He knew him before he was even known as Jeremiah, before conception, meaning he was born for this very role that the LORD had prearranged for him to walk into. And so, it is also for you and me. He's calling us because we were created for that calling.

All this while, God knew me and had His plans for my life, with nothing to compare to what I had in mind for myself. Because at this age, I wasn't yet thinking of what I wanted to become, and I knew nothing about destiny. His plans are far beyond what my mind could have ever imagined. I pray this prayer for you and me. From this day forward, you will tap into that calling, and those plans He has for you and has appointed for you will be manifested in Jesus' mighty name, amen.

Introduction

When the LORD, wants to use us, when He wants to achieve something through us, we must be obedient to His voice. We must understand it is not about us. It's not about our own abilities, our own strength, it's simply about obedience. As a Christian, I struggled in this area for years. I thought I was not good enough, not educated enough, not Christian enough. I used to say, "Oh LORD, are You sure You want to use me?" I doubted everything the LORD said to me about myself. I questioned it for years. I mean, I questioned it to the point I began laughing at God. I thought it was funny. I simply thought I wasn't capable, little did I know that was true. I was not capable on my own. It was not until I started praying and seeking God to gain a better understanding of what He was saying to me and how He wanted me to go about this "walking in destiny," that I began to understand what it means to be called by the LORD. It means He wants to use me as His own voice on earth to reach other young women who look, sound, and have experienced similar things just like me, a vessel He wants to work through.

The LORD did not save me to run around and play a cute Christian living a mediocre life. I began to realize He saved me to send me back out to rescue young women who look, sound, and have experiences like me. He wants to send me out to go to war, to be a sheep amongst wolves. He validates me so that when I walk into any room, I will not look for a man to validate me, but simply rely on His approval. Why He wants to work through me I don't know, and I will probably never really understand. But for now, I know He wants to use me. "Here I am LORD—do Your will through me."

Understanding what He really means for me and wants me to do is not about what I can do but realizing what I am capable of doing with Him within me. As I prayed each day for the LORD to give me the power to just trust Him, things began to shift. You may not know where He is leading you, in fact, most of the time you will not know where He is leading you, but the point is you must trust Him.

The LORD promises us He will never lead us astray. He only wants to lead us to our destiny, our calling, our Victory. In Joshua 1:5 the LORD reminds Joshua that just like He was with Moses, who was before him in leading his people into the promised land, so He will be with Joshua. "No man shall *be able* to stand before you all the days of your life; as I was with Moses, so I will be with you. I will not leave you nor forsake you" (NKJV). You ought to know He is with you as you obey Him and walk with Him to achieve whatever He's trying to achieve through you. You may not be leading people into a strange new land like Joshua, but that calling He's trying to achieve through you is not for you but for His glory.

Walking into your destiny requires you to be in alignment with God. This will only happen when you start to live in the Word of God, when you begin to dig deeper. The Word is your manual; it has all the instructions you need to walk you through each day of your life and through your journey. It is your GPS, giving you turn-by-turn navigation information, travel tips, and route details.

Growing Up

Train up a child in the way he should go: and when he is old, he will not depart from it."

Proverbs 22:6

Before all of this, I was just a little ole girl born to Fula parents who are still Muslim and still follow their traditional beliefs. I am praying that soon and very soon that they too will come to know the LORD and be set free. I was born in the Northern Province of Sierra Leone, Tonkolili District, Magburaka, where 99 percent of Sierra Leonean Fulas are Muslim. Of course, as a child, I had to follow my family religious practices, so I practiced the Muslim faith mixed with traditional beliefs, as most Fula people in Sierra Leone do.

Adherents believe in ancestral spirits and the supernatural, sacrifices, and rituals. I can recall as a child, washing with different types of water and rubbing on different types of remedies for protection and blessings, so they taught us. Now, these were all meant for our good, so my parents thought. As the Bible tells us in Hosea 4:6, "for lack of knowledge my people perish," my parents were unknowingly partaking in doings that were set up to destroy me later. Doings that later manifested in me in the forms of anger, rage, and sexual immorality. But they thought they were protecting their little girl through these practices.

I supposed this was the way of believing in a higher being, which I was learning from my parents, and they had also learned from their parents and so on. I believe that my parents saw their beliefs as a way of life that was transmitted between generations and they considered it part of their parenting to pass on their faith to their children. Looking back now as a follower of Christ, I can see that my grandparents did not understand that the transmission of religious values was a way of providing direction for their children and grandchildren and creating a strong base on which they could build their lives. This made it very hard for them to be open to anything else, such as salvation.

At the age of five I began nursery school, which is known as kindergarten in the United States. I was also enrolled in Arabic nursery school. I remember going to school in the mornings on the back of my father's okada (motorcycle). This was my favorite part of going to school. My father faithfully took me to school when he was not on one of his many business trips. After nursery school, my father would pick me up and take me to our family shop to hang out until it was dusk when we would go to Arabic nursery school. Going to Arabic school we learned the basics of how to pray and read the surahs in the Quran.

The five daily prayers are amongst the most important acts of worship that Muslims perform. It is considered a great sin to neglect the five daily prayers, so my parents instilled this belief in us at a young age, hoping it would stick with us all the days of our lives. Just as I later learned what the Bible says in the book of Proverbs, "Train up a child in the way he should go: and when he is old, he will not depart from it" (Proverbs 22:6). There were great intentions and great initiatives. Taking my prayer life seriously was a great trait I learned from my parents and has helped me a great deal, especially now. They wanted to set us up for the future, to make sure we were equipped for whatever life would throw at us, I later realized.

Arabic school is mostly about memorization. My parents recognized that engaging their children in religious activities would have a significant part to play in shaping our faith identity. It was just unfortunate that their way of religion isn't the way of salvation. Not to mention, their "faith" was nothing more than the religious practices passed down to them by their parents. They recognized that parents have a significant part to play in shaping the faith identity of their children and engaging them in religious activities.

See, when I was a little girl my father had two wives. These were the days I heard and saw my parents fight the most. It seemed to me that no matter what my mother did, my father was never happy with her. My mother, being the first wife, wanted her husband to herself of course and did not want to share him with the other woman. The other woman came into the family after I was born. I have two sisters who are the same age but only a couple of months apart. Because of this, both wives fought for my father's attention.

Based on their religious beliefs, they turned to what we call a "Moray man" to do voodoo on their husband to win his attention. The voodoo was meant to make him love one wife and despise the other. This went on for years, one wife would put the voodoo she got from the moray man in my father's food and when he ate the meal, depending on who is doing the voodoo, he would start to despise the other wife. So, he would be in love with one wife for a week but turn on her the next week when it was the other wife's turn to have the husband. Then she would cook for him and feed him whatever she got from the moray man. My mother and the second wife turned against each other, they hated one another—hate so strong they wanted to destroy each other and everything the other represented. Who knows, if the children from both marriages didn't suffer some of that "moray man voodoo" they were both involved in. Not to mention some of the difficulties I faced later in life and needed the LORD to deliver me.

I remember seeing my father with one wife for a week at a time then rotate to the next wife. This went on for years. On the day either wife was with him, that wife was very happy. Whoever was with the husband was responsible for cooking and doing household chores. On my mother's week, she was happy and jovial. She would wake up with a smile on her face, laughing and interacting with her children. My mother has a jolly, bubbly and very funny personality. When she was happy, we had the most fun. She is the kind of person who could make you laugh so hard your head hurts from one temple to the other side of your head. Despite the many changes that occurred during this time with the two wives, my mother always made us laugh. 'Til this day, she is as playful as I can remember. To me, it's one of her greatest attributes as a mother. You know, looking back now, it was silly for my father to honestly think he could keep two women happy under one roof, not to mention the three girls he had at the time. Five females under one roof and he knew each wife was only for her own children.

My father had a very soft spot for his little girls, but I have to say especially for me since I was his first child. He never allowed his problematic wives to get in the way of his relationship with his daughters. Whatever we wanted Daddy got us. We had him wrapped around our little fingers. He never treated us differently based on what was going on with the wives. He somehow knew how to separate the two. He knew how to love his daughters and kept us happy.

Of course growing up, I did not like seeing my mother sad because of rotating my father around, but most importantly, I did not like seeing her fight for her husband's attention knowing the other woman was the cause of her sadness and desperation. My mother was married to my father first; they were married for years before the second wife came about.

My parents were very strict but were also very caring and loving. They applied harsh punishments when the rules were broken, but they were also very generous with their children and always praised us. Since my parents did not really go to school, they wanted us to be educated. It was very important that we got good grades and got into the best secondary school in the country. Schools in Sierra Leone graded students based on a ranking scale. So, if there were twenty students in a classroom the rank will be from first place to twentieth place and of course when we were students in primary school (which is considered elementary school here in the United States) our parents always made it very clear we are were not allowed to rank less

8

than the fifth in our classes. That was a lot of pressure for a little girl. But it equipped us for success and we always had a private tutor who came to the house to help us with homework or any areas we might have been weak in.

We were very sheltered compared to other children in our neighborhood, my parents were very strict, as I mentioned, but they were also very caring and loving. My parents were easily sterner than all my friend's parents. Muslim parents are normally more exacting than non-Muslim parents. Even though we were not required to wear hijabs daily, other than before praying, we only wore modest clothing. Back then even my mother was not allowed to wear pants or jeans. She wears them now but as I was growing up my father did not let her wear pants. Of Course, we wore pants, but our school uniforms were loose dresses that passed below our knees and midway down our legs.

As Muslim girls, we were not allowed to date under any circumstances. Now, as a mother of an elementary-age child, I often see kids starting to date in elementary schools here in the United States and the parents agree to it. As a child born to Muslim Fula parents, this was unheard of. No boyfriends and that was that— point-blank period, no room for explanation. As for sleepovers, that did not happen in our household. We could have only female friends who came over to play with us in our enclosed yard. Since there was just one television in the home, we only watched movies with parental supervision. We did not play any sports, sports were considered a boy thing. We were not allowed to even ride bikes, as it was not considered safe for girls. We were required to limit the amount of time spent with boys to whom we were not related. So, we did not interact much with boys at all.

Even though we stayed in our yard to play, when we were growing up everybody knew everyone else. Any adult who knew us had the right to discipline us. Which meant we couldn't hide or get away with anything. You could just forget about it. Everyone knew you by your kin, and you were known as someone's daughter, sister, granddaughter, cousin, and so on. Yes, it may sound like everyone was always in your private life, but there was something special about growing up in a small town. It was not until our move to the United States, I realized how special it was to come from a place like that. There was something special about experiencing childhood in a town where people knew you and cared about you. A place where, if you wanted to, you could run around town under the stars that weren't hidden by skyscrapers and know you would be safe.

Somewhere in all this, there was also a civil war that took place in Sierra Leone that lasted eleven years. I remember moving from one city to the other, hiding from rebels. Most of the rebels were young men who had been captured and forced to be child soldiers. Some of my male cousins were captured and made child soldiers. My very first-time hearing of the war as a child was one evening just after dinner. One of my aunts ran into our house with her hands on her head, sobbing. She began shouting, "They took him, they took him, what am I going to do? My son is gone, he's going to be turned into one of them. He's going to be a rebel."

Some weeks later we were attacked. Rebels broke into our home and asked everyone to put their hands up and lay on the floor. We were horrified. Thankfully they were only interested in looting, they took what they wanted and left. But as they were leaving our house my mother spotted my cousin who was amongst them. They were all wearing facemasks but somehow, she recognized him as they walked away. This was a common thing, they would capture a young man and have that young man take them to his family members' homes to loot anything they could find to fund themselves.

The constant moving continued for a while. My father was in the mining industry, which was a very hot place for the rebels. The rebels took control of as many diamond mines as possible, forcing civilians to work in the mines and sell the diamonds to earn money for their military. As depicted in the 2006 movie, *Blood Diamond,* the diamonds were sold to fuel the war.

After some time, running and hiding from the rebels in the provinces my father decided to move the family into the city, Freetown. I'm not sure what happened to the second wife and her daughter, but by the move to Freetown, she was not around. At this point, it was just my father, mother, brother, two sisters, and myself. I believe during the time we were hiding from the rebels she went away with her child. So that was the end of the two-wife situation, from this point on my mother was the only wife.

Off we went to Freetown. My father's older sister and her family lived in Freetown and of course, we stayed with them. For some reason there were no rebels in Freetown yet, so we were very happy. After having stopped going to school during the race of running and hiding for our lives we started back to school again. Life seemed to start getting back to normal so, we stayed in Freetown.

The civil war was a brutal war in which hundreds of thousands of Sierra Leoneans were unnecessarily killed, wounded and mutilated.

In 2001, things got even better when my father received a call one evening from a very good friend, who shared the great news of his girls winning the DV lottery. On May 9, 2002, we arrived in the United States—a new land, new opportunities, new challenges. Since our parents were not part of the program, it was just my little sister and me and another group of people. We had to find a place to live in the U.S. After a long search we found out one of our aunts lived In Columbus, Ohio, and we went to live with her We stayed in Ohio for three years, throughout our middle school years, before moving to Virginia. My aunt also had a male family friend who she was helping. He was staying with her until he got on his feet.

The day we arrived in the United States it was somewhat chilly. Coming from 90-degree weather all our lives and considering our very light African attire it felt like the temperature was below zero. We were not dressed for the weather we walked into. In Sierra Leone, the climate is tropical, hot all year round. Adjusting to the change in climate was just one of the many challenges we faced in the United States.

The first and foremost challenge that every immigrant must face is the culture shock. The way things are done in America is definitely different from the way things are done in Sierra Leone. The culture, the atmosphere, and the people are all different. But then again, I often thought to myself, *But isn't that why we came here? For the change?* I did not criticize, I tried to adjust. Communication was one of the biggest challenges I faced. It was not so much a language barrier as it was the difficulty of people understanding my very thick African accent.

Being from a developing (a.k.a. third-world) country did not mean we could not speak English. We spoke English just fine, so we thought until we entered middle school. Every word that came out of my mouth into the middle schoolers' ears must have sounded like Kevin Hart on stage at a stand-up comedy show. They laughed at every word that came out of my mouth; for some reason, my accent was as funny as a comedian to them. To be quite honest, at first, I was really confused. I often wondered why they laughed every time I opened my mouth to speak. They also sounded different to me, but I never once thought to laugh or tease them or embarrass them.

I could not wrap my thoughts around the fact that the kids who laughed at me were the same ones who looked like me, the African American kids. Where I came from, America was known as the white man's country. On the first day of school, I was so happy to see other kids who looked like me, but instead, my happiness turned into shame. The African-American kids laughed at me the most. I often wondered, *Why do they laugh at me when in fact they look just like me?* One day on the bus I just got fed up with all the teasing decided one day to take matters into my own hands. I ended up getting suspended from school for some time. The girl's family even threatened to take me to court but it never went that far. It's so interesting to see how now, being from a different part of the world is starting to become a plus, even in the workforce. Being bi-lingual is a bonus, people celebrate different ethnicities now.

In 2005, the summer before we entered high school, my aunt moved to New Jersey and we had to move to Northern Virginia to stay with our cousin who had just gotten married and was starting a family. Northern Virginia is often referred to as a mixing bowl, where you can find every ethnic group you could imagine. At this point, my so-very-thick African accent was starting to fade away. In Virginia, it is very common to find people renting out empty rooms in their homes since the cost of living is so expensive. So, as I mentioned, my cousins had male roommates who were renting a room from them. When we came on board, there was still enough room to have roommates and live comfortably. So that continued.

At this point I'd had a growth spurt and was beginning to look more like a woman, growing fat in the right places—my hips were starting to widen, and breasts were growing. I started dating, my first official relationship happened in high school, a time when most adolescents are hyped on hormones and their brains are not fully developed yet. Through the years I've learned that first relationships are like tornados, guaranteed to do some damage.

I attended T. C. Williams High School throughout my high school years. It is a public high school in Alexandria, Virginia, just minutes from Washington. D.C. It is a very large school, as a matter of fact; it's the only high school in Alexandria City with an enrollment of about 3,800 students. Students there are from all ethnic groups. The motion picture, *Remember the Titans,* was about T. C. Williams consolidating into one high school in 1971, which also meant that it was desegregated. I was fortunate to have attended a school with a 79-percent total minority enrollment.

T.C. Williams offers lots of Advanced Placement courses and vocational training programs. So in my senior year, I took the Licensed Practical nursing program. But this program had two phases, which meant that after my senior year I had to return for the second phase to complete the program and take a National Council Licensure Examination to become a Licensed Practical Nurse.

While all my friends were talking about applying to colleges and planning life after high school, I was faced with the decision to return to high school to complete this program. To be honest, I did not want to complete the program. I wanted to go off to college like the rest of my friends, but the reality was I did not have the money to go off to college. I ended up speaking with the program director, who talked some sense into my head, and I made the decision to stay and complete the program. This is where my love for nursing started. I finished the program, took the exam, and became an LPN.

Growing up I encountered many challenges, but little did I know that at the end of it all God was going to work it all out for my good. From the tropical life of Sierra Leone to the skyscrapers and winter life in the United States, I have to say I am blessed to have been able to experience my childhood in such different places with such grace and joy. Yes, there was lots of adapting that took place, which made me the woman I am becoming today. I say, "becoming," because I do not think I am quite where I need to be yet. You know, one of the greatest things I have learned is that living a fulfilled and destined life is not a destination at all, it's a journey that requires consistency and constant growth. We must be open to improvement and growth even when we might think we have arrived at our calling.

Can't Tell a Soul

In Islam, sex before marriage is absolutely forbidden. You are to stay untouched, a virgin until marriage. Growing up, having a boyfriend was out of the equation. I knew it and knew that I was going to stay a virgin until marriage. As a matter of fact, we did not even have male friends much less boyfriends. We were only to have close interactions with males in our family such as brothers, cousins, or very close family friends. As a little girl, I knew that I was going to follow this mandate. Being obedient to our parents was very important, we did as they said without question.

Every parent's dream is to raise their children in the way they know to be righteous and one day see them grow up into adults and be proud to see everything good they have instilled in them. Now that I am a parent myself, I understand the importance of being able to protect and guide your children. I believe this whole thing about staying a virgin until marriage was a way to protect our innocence. Even though parents cannot always protect the innocence of their children they know one fact is for certain: If a child loses innocence about a certain thing too early, and the child is not yet mature enough to fully grasp what that thing is, the outcome is usually frightful. My parents tried to guard my innocence by instilling values in me and surrounding us with trusted people.

Despite my parents' efforts, the thought of being untouched was completely destroyed at the age of eight for me. My very first encounter with exploring my genital organs started one night while I was deep asleep in a room shared with two other girls. In Africa, sharing a room with family members and sleeping on the same bed with family members of the same gender is very common. So, we shared beds, the normal thing to do. We had been sharing a bed for a while now without any problems. But one night I woke up from my sleep by a touch I had never felt before. I felt a hand in my underwear moving, searching for something. So, when I woke up my natural defense mechanism kicked in and I quickly moved the hand. I went back to sleep, but I woke up that morning wondering to myself what that was all about. I kept it to myself and did not tell anyone, but I thought about it a lot. I went on to school that morning as usual, but I found myself just staring into space, thinking about what had happened. At one point the teacher came to my desk and bent down to eye level and looked at me, she knew something was wrong. She asked if I was okay. "Of course," I replied, and told her that I was just tired from not sleeping well the night before.

For the entire school day, she paid close attention to me, because I was usually one of the talkative students who she constantly had to ask to stop talking. This day, however, I was very quiet, and she knew I was not my normal self. Due to the concern and care she showed, I considered telling her what had happened but for some reason every time I thought I might tell her the thought of not telling my parents first kept creeping in my head. I kept thinking to myself that if I did not tell my parents first, they would be very upset if they heard it from my teacher and not me, so I just kept it to myself.

When the school day ended and it was time to go home, my heart was racing. I was so nervous to go home I was shaking. But I went, fighting my feelings and thoughts all the way there because I knew if I didn't hide them my mother would notice my behavior and would get to the bottom of it. When I got there, I lied and said I wasn't well and needed to eat and go to bed early. But I had to share a bed with the other girls and fear crept in. But I went on to bed anyway and since I was the only one on the bed, I fell asleep quickly. I didn't feel anything during the night, so when I woke up and I was so happy and relieved. I went to school and I was back to my normal self, talking and interacting with my classmates as usual. When my teacher saw that I was back to my talkative self she believed that I was just tired the day before She even suggested that I start going to bed earlier to help me get more rest at night.

A week went by and at that point, I thought it was just a onetime thing and was so glad it had not happened again. I remember being so relieved that it seemed it was not going to be a repeated act. That wonderful feeling of relief lasted another three days. This time it was different. She had her hand in my underwear again and was trying to open my legs with her other hand. She was whispering in my ear, telling me to "shhh." She said, "Don't be afraid. It's ok, I promise you will like it, it feels good." She kept saying, "You are going to wake the other girl up if you don't be quiet. Just open your legs, I am trying to make you feel good."

I was so shocked and traumatized I tensed my body and just laid there in tears. As she continued, I sobbed even more. Then suddenly I just became numb to it all and was very calm. This went on for several minutes before she realized I was not enjoying the act as she thought I would. So, she stopped and said, "Don't worry, you will get used to it. It's supposed to feel good. It only hurts now because it's your first time." After saying that she laid down and got ready to go back to sleep.

But before she did, she gave me the threat of my life: She told me not to tell a soul and that if I did tell anyone and she found out she would somehow make sure it all fell on me. I laid there for the rest of the night and could not make myself fall asleep. My tears were continuously soaking the pillow. She went back to sleep as if nothing had happened. It was the longest night of my life. As the sun rose in the morning I slowly got up and walked out of the room with my head down. I felt like I was dead, like someone had sucked the life out of me. I felt bad but interestingly, I wasn't in a panic. I could not understand why I was so calm. I went and took my shower as usual and somehow it felt like all my emotions were washed away. I went about my normal activities before I started my walk to school. My school was within walking distance and I daily walked to and from with friends. This time I was not daydreaming like I was the first time when my teacher noticed straight away that something was wrong. I was very cheerful and acted as if nothing had happened. That was my way of dealing with it at the time. I figured that if I pretended as if nothing had happened then everything would be just fine and nobody would notice.

From that point on, every night at about the same time the ritual continued. She would be in my underwear night after night to the point where I became numb to it. I woke up every morning like nothing happened, took my shower, got ready, and walked to school. My mother never noticed a change in my behavior as I was always my cheerful self during breakfast. I felt like I didn't even have to pretend because it almost felt like the happy mask was my own. It was the same every day and every night: I laid there and allowed her to do what she did, then I got up in the morning as if nothing had happened. During the act, I never felt okay with it but I lived my life as if I were okay. There were times I wondered if she was doing the same thing to my other cousin. I could never really tell by just looking at her. Maybe she was pretending like I was. I hid it well. It was a part of life I guess, to the point where she would say time after time, "It feels good, right?" I never responded to her—I was always very quiet. She would say, "I know you like it that's why you're not saying anything." Then one night she said, "They said it feels better when you're not circumcised, you better enjoy it."

I never really understood what she meant and was just too numb to even say anything. It wasn't until I got a bit older that I came to understand that some girls, depending on their parents' beliefs, were circumcised.

She used many different tactics to manipulate me to stay quiet. She said things like, "If you tell I'll turn it all on you. Nobody is going to believe you anyway so you better not even try it, you will end up getting in trouble for not telling the first time. Plus, I know you like it so if you want to continue feeling good you better not tell, or it will all be over." For some reason, she did all the talking. I never responded to her. I just listened. I was intimidated by her, she was older and to me, she was smart and could outsmart me if I even thought about telling on her. So, I was afraid to tell. Plus, I knew I would for sure get in trouble for not telling the first time—why tell now?

She acted as if it was normal and as if I enjoyed it. There were times I tried to refuse by closing my legs but every time I tried, she would threaten to tell my parents that I was doing what she was doing to me. I was so fearful of the thought of my parents hearing that I was participating in any sexual activity that I just let her do what she wanted to do night after night.

One time my mother almost caught me because I was walking awkwardly, but when she started to question me, I told her it was because my stomach hurt. She knew I could not tolerate pain at all. So as usual, she gave me medication and told me to lie down and rest. My mother is the kind of mother who would do anything to make sure her children were safe. For her to know such a thing was happening to her little girl would have devastated her so, I tried even harder to hide it from her especially since my father traveled a lot as a businessman anyway.

One night I was lying in bed, but I was not asleep, one of my many sleepless nights. I anticipated the usual activity, but I noticed she did not wake up so I was getting excited thinking maybe I was off the hook. That one night she slept, but the next night it was back to it again. They were unending, painful episodes that became invasive over time. I was so disappointed. It went on again and again non-stop. Because of the situation, I became overly concerned and protective of my younger siblings. I started taking the role of a caretaker even though I was a kid myself. I did not tell them what was going on even though I often wondered if someone was doing the same thing to them.

I recall people always saying I was very mature for my age. I was forced to keep the sexual abuse a secret, which made me feel trapped and helpless. Powerless. I did not want any of my siblings to ever feel the same way, so I began playing the big sister role. I knew if I had a trusted relationship with them if anything like what I was experiencing ever happened to them they would hopefully tell me.

One day my father came home from a long trip and said we were moving to the next section of the building. Oh boy, was I happy! My face lit up! My father noticed the excitement on my face and made a comment: "I thought you guys liked it here." I quickly replied and said, "Yes, we do, but it will be nice to have more space."

Moving day came and we moved practically next door, but to me, it seemed as if we were moving across the globe. It seemed like enough distance to protect me from being violated any more. It was such a huge relief. Knowing I did not have to share a room with the perpetrator any longer was like winning the lottery. My heart was filled with joy. I was off the hook. I was off the hook of manipulation, violation, and exploitation. I was free from captivity and torture. I was so happy to know I did not have to pretend anymore. I was going to be a normal little girl again.

For the first few nights, I woke up in a slight panic. My body seemed to be used to waking up about the same time each night in anticipation of being violated. Eventually, I started regaining peace again. I went to bed in peace and woke up in peace; it felt so good to not have to worry about someone taking advantage of my body every night.

Whenever I saw my cousin, I would have flashbacks. They were so vivid I would hide from her and try to stay away from her as much as I could. It was difficult because we all lived in the same compound and I could only hide so much. I saw her daily and we had to interact. I could not act differently, because then someone would notice my behavior and that would have been a problem. She never mentioned it and we both pretended as if nothing had happened, but my mind was well aware of what had happened. I could not stop thinking about the violation whenever I saw her. Fortunately, it was only when

I saw her though. That was better than reliving it every night.

After a couple of months of being in our own area of the compound, my dad came back from one of his trips and brought one of his nephews from the village. He said he was going to stay with us and go to school in the city. We call our cousins brothers and sisters, so my parents would refer to us as sisters and brothers. One night as we were sleeping in our room this brother of mine came into the room pretending to look for something in the middle of the night, but I was not fully asleep yet. I felt someone walk in the room, but I was too tired to wake up or make a sound.

He stood over my sisters and me as we were lying there and then he tried lying next to me. At that point, my heart was racing and all I could think to my self was, *Not again*. So, I did not move. I pretended I was sleeping. But he moved his hand toward my underwear and I hit him hard and I screamed, but by the time my father came out to see what was going on he had fled. Thankfully, my father believed me when I told him what had happened. He told him to leave the house immediately and go over to the other complex where my cousins were and said that they would discuss it in the morning. My parents concluded that maybe he should just stay at the other complex but not with us.

The move to the United States was a great relief for me. Not only were we going to be in the land of opportunity, but I also knew I was going to be completely free from the mental exhaustion of the sexual exploitation I had experienced. Or so I thought. As mentioned earlier, there was a family friend who had also won the DV lottery and was staying with us at my aunt's house when we arrived. We lived in a family-friendly suburban neighborhood. Not many African were in this area at the time, we were the only Africans on the entire block. But I liked it a lot in Columbus, it was very quiet and peaceful which reminded me of most evenings in Sierra Leone. It was peaceful at dusk. My aunt worked the typical nine-to-five schedule Monday through Friday, so every morning she would get ready and head to work. Since we had to wait for our documents to process before we could start school, we stayed home for a couple of weeks. Our family friend also had to wait for his work permit to come before he could start job hunting.

During this waiting period, my aunt would leave my sister and me with him as a trusted adult to watch over us while she was at work. It was not long before he started his episodes of sexual exploration and exploitation. I used to be an early riser. I would wake up very early before my sister was up to watch my favorite Disney Channel shows on TV and he noticed that. Most of the time when my aunt was leaving for work I would be the only one up. She would always remind me not to open the door for anyone and to always get an adult if someone was at the door. One morning my Aunt went to work as usual and he came in the living room as I was sitting on the couch watching my show. He sat right next to me. Once again, my heart starting racing and I was breathing very hard. He noticed it and asked, "What's wrong with you? Are you afraid of me?"

I looked down and was silent. He said, "It's okay. I am not going to hurt you. Wait, I'll show you. It's okay, I will not hurt you." He forced his hand in my pants and in my underwear. I thought to myself, *Why me? Not again, I thought this was over with.* I had flown across the ocean to a different environment, a different continent and it still followed me. After this incident, I started thinking it was my fault. Maybe there was something I was doing that was provoking these people to do this to me. I shut down, and my countenance changed. An overwhelming feeling of sadness came upon me. I sat there completely numb until he was done with what he was doing. He got up and left the room when he noticed my little sister was up.

I laid on the couch not knowing what to do. *What do I do?* I thought to myself. I did not want to tell my little sister about what had happened, so I laid there and pretended to be asleep. As I laid there, I thought of telling my aunt. She had given us her cell phone and work number in the event of an emergency. She also taught us how to call the police, but I thought, *If I tell her she will immediately leave work and come home, and I did not want to make a big scene.* For God's sake, we had just arrived! We were all lost and confused. I was just trying to learn and adjust to the new environment. So, I did not tell. My aunt came home, and I hid it well, so she did not notice a thing.

Weeks went by and the abuse continued. Every night I would go to bed blaming myself for it all. Even though I could not think of one thing I had done wrong I continued to blame myself. Almost two months went by as he continued. He only did it when my aunt was at work. One day, God gave me the strength to pick up the phone as soon as he was done. I waited until he was outside in the yard and then I called my aunt. I remember crying on the phone and she somehow knew something was very wrong and came home immediately. When she came home, I explained everything to her and off he went. My aunt paid for a hotel for him that day and bought him a ticket to leave Ohio and go to New Jersey to stay with another family member. I never laid eyes on him again.

Life went on. In the typical African household once something is taken care of we never really talk about it again. Since he was gone, as far as I knew the problem was solved. Life went on. I struggled with flashbacks for a while as I started school, but I kept it all to myself. I had more important things like my accent to deal with and the teasing at school so flashbacks were the least of my worries. I was just so glad he was gone. I was hopeful that one day the flashbacks, too, would subside. Whenever I was in the middle of a flashback I would tell myself, *It's over, he is gone,* and would try to distract myself by looking around and counting things around me or saying the names of things I saw in the room. That helped me a lot. I strongly believe that God was the One guiding me in how to deal with the emotional disturbance during those times. Eventually, the flashbacks stopped.

In the summer of 2005, my Aunt moved to New Jersey and we had to go live with my older cousin who lived in Northern Virginia. She had just gotten married and was starting her family. Right in the neighborhood we lived in we saw people who sounded and looked just like us. Our first summer in Virginia felt like Sierra Leone, it was hot. I liked that. We had so much fun during the summer. we went out to African events where we got to mingle with other Sierra Leoneans. I met some of my cousins and saw people I knew from back home. Alexandria felt like a mini Sierra Leone for a moment.

Due to the very expensive cost of living in Northern Virginia, renting an empty room in one's home is very common. Of Course, my older cousin and her husband had a couple of male roommates who were renting from them. Their home was big enough to house us all, even with the roommates so there was no need to ask them to vacate. But one of the roommates would always stare me down and made me very uncomfortable. At this point, I was about fifteen and this roommate was probably in his late twenties or early thirties.

In northern Virginia, there were lots of snow days when we would have no school, unlike Ohio where we went to school no matter how many feet of snow there was. This was different for us, so on the days it snowed, we stayed home for the most part. Sometimes when we had snow days this roommate would also be home and would try talking to me, making small talk here and there. He would ask things like, "How's school? How do you like it here in Virginia? You made new friends yet?" Just enough to start a conversation. He never really talked about anything of importance. I started noticing this behavior, then it became a pattern. He would be home every time we had no school due to snow. It went from him being there sometimes to him being home every time we had no school. I started becoming suspicious.

In the middle of that winter, I was forced to lose my virginity. He raped me that morning when everyone was gone to work. My little sister was in the room sleeping and I was walking into the bathroom.

He came and grabbed me by my hand and pulled me in his room, which was next to the bathroom which we shared. He pushed me on the bed and forced himself on me. I laid there in shock and pain. I laid there for a while then suddenly, this strength came over me and I pushed him off and ran out of the room. I went into the bathroom and took the longest shower I have ever taken in my life. I kept it to myself. I thought, *Why should I even bother telling this time, it must be me and telling only gets rid of the person until someone else comes along for it to repeat itself all over again.* So, I went on with life. I hid it and never told anyone.

I felt like all my life I was in circumstances where I had to second-guess whether to tell or not. Then even when I told it only stopped for a while, the abuse would inevitably start up again. I moved quite a bit—from Africa to America, from Ohio to Virginia, and it followed me wherever I went. I was the problem. *How could all these people be the problem? What was I doing wrong?* I asked these questions for years. I blamed myself but could never figure out why it always happened to me. I lived in self-blame and that is why I never told a soul. Losing my virginity to rape was against everything I thought about sex. I was only fifteen and not married for sure, and now not a virgin; what a disgrace. I was so embarrassed. I knew one day I would have to explain how I lost my virginity. For some, the day they lose their virginity is a beautiful and important day. For me, I prayed that I would completely forget that day. Somehow, I couldn't erase the memory, it was permanent, and I had to learn how to live with it.

The Bully

Take my yoke upon you, and learn of me; for I am meek and lowly in heart: and ye shall find rest unto your souls.

Matthew 11:29

Immediately after the incident, I went through a roller coaster of feelings and emotions. I'm not sure how it happened, but eventually, I found the strength to ignore it and just enough courage to hide it like so many girls and women do every day around the world. Silence was my shield. Some sort of transformation took place in me that I did not quite understand at the time. Somehow in the process of leaving the memory behind me, bullying others became my way of covering the psychological trauma.

At the time, it was a way of controlling my mind. If I made fun of others, often very close friends, and saw how it affected them and hurt them, then that made me feel better about myself. I only targeted very close friends, because since they were my friends, I felt that they did not see it as bullying. You know the saying, "Real friends will tell you the truth about yourself." Well, I sure abused that phrase. I used to say things like, "I tell it as I see it. I am not afraid to tell you about yourself. It's better to have someone tell you that cares enough to tell you the truth." I thought, *Oh well, it not my fault she looks like that, I'm only letting her know because it's the truth.* I told myself anything to justify my behavior.

My two closest friends were my main punching bags. On days when I dealt with flashbacks, I lashed out at them, and of course, they had no idea what I was battling within my mind. They could only tell me, I was very mean to them on certain days. It wasn't all the time, just on days I needed to make myself feel better. They were very close to me; we did everything together. The little we were permitted to do anyway, as we were all from African households. Our families

27

were very strict. We were not allowed to participate in many of the activates that took place in high school. Things like going to games or parties were simply out of the equation. We were, however, allowed to go to supervised school activities like school dances and field trips.

To make up for the lack of freedom we used to stay after school almost every day, claiming our teachers were helping us in areas we were weak in. I used to say that I was staying after school with my math teacher for extra help since I was not doing well in that subject. Sometimes we did stay on school premises just hanging out but most days we went to the mall or just walked around the neighborhood until it was time to go home. There was this high-rise apartment building that we considered very fancy. It had all the amenities and we used to go into their gymnasium and sit on their machines and talk for hours as if we lived there. There was a mirrored wall and we loved standing there just looking at ourselves as we talked to each other.

We talked about the normal teenage things, the boys we had a crush on, who's dating who, fashion, our insecurities, our bodies, and our struggles. At that age, of course, identity is a big struggle for everyone. So, we would look at ourselves in the mirror, pointing out parts on our bodies we liked and parts we did not like so much. For instance, I would always look at my butt, my hips, and my breasts. I was obsessed with my body and used it to make fun of my friends' still-developing bodies. I was womanly shaped at an early age. Extra adipose tissue had developed on my hips, thighs, and buttocks as a teenage girl to the point where even boys noticed and would call me "big body girl." I took that as a compliment and was full of myself. I thought I was all that plus so much more.

Looking in the mirror at our bodies, I would often point out to them how I had the perfect body and how they wished they looked like me. I would step back so they could have a good view of me with my hands waving up and down, taunting them, "Look at this body! It's all-natural, you wish you had a body like this! I'm sorry you look like that, I have the perfect body and you don't." Interestingly enough, they never really said a thing. They just looked at me in silence. The looks they gave me made me feel they agreed with me that I did look better than they did. That made me feel even better about myself. Knowing they agreed with the fact that my body was perfect made me feel superior. It was my new way of coping with the torment of my terrible past. It was my way of making myself feel higher, by bringing them down. But honestly, because I felt so low myself, I wanted to make them feel as low as I was feeling inside, and I fed off that. It was not a healthy way of coping, but it was my coping mechanism at the time. Bullies bully others to make themselves feel better and I did just that to the people who were closest to me.

Even though I was mean to both, one friend suffered from the bulling the most. Since she was unsure of herself and had low self-esteem, I noticed it and targeted her. I did what every bully does: Attack people who appear weak and vulnerable. This friend I attacked the most was sensitive about her body. She made it known she was not happy with herself and with that in mind, I made her my main target.

We fought a lot. There was always tension between us. Looking back now, we had so much in common and that's why we bumped heads the most, it was a love/hate relationship. We would be the best of friends one minute and the next would be fighting and calling each other names. We were emotionally ill, and we were both looking for some sort of validation. I am not sure what she was battling but looking back I'm sure she also was suffering within, just like me.

I was really mean to her, I even called her "pizza face" to embarrass her in front of others. Of Course, as a teenager, I did not understand her acne was just because of the increase of androgens, sex hormones, causing an excess of oil gland secretion. All I saw was pimples everywhere, raised red spots with white centers and so "pizza face" seemed appropriate. I called her other names too, but she hated that one the most. Due to the name-calling, she began wearing heavy make-up to cover up her face. Most women these days would tell you they wear make-up because it's fun and it makes them feel more confident. She wore makeup not only to make herself feel more confident but most importantly she wore it because of the naming calling. The make-up did cover the pimples, but that did not stop me from the name-calling. I continued to call her "pizza face."

I also called her fat a lot, too. Size-wise she was bigger than me, but she wasn't fat. Because she looked bigger than I was I thought that made her fat and I used it to belittle her. For teenagers, the go-to insult is the three-letter word, "fat." Regardless of how much she weighed calling her fat made her believe she was indeed fat, and she also started calling herself fat. I threw lots of insults at her; I judged her, criticized her, and humiliated her almost every day. Most of the time she just looked at me and never tried to defend herself. It may have been said that people call others out on their weight because they are secretly concerned about their own size, but that was no the case for me, it was only a way of patronizing and humiliating her. Sometimes I would say to her, "You know if you did not eat so much maybe you would not be so fat."

As teenagers we loved food, I would say we ate a lot. We loved fast food especially. On days we had money to spend after walking around after school we would go get fast food and eat before going home. I always had some sort of cash on me because I used to do hair and made money that way on the weekends. I was generous enough to buy my friends food, but only what I wanted to get them. I would tell them to pick something less than five dollars but then would get whatever I wanted since it was my money and not theirs. They were always grateful for whatever I got them and never complained that I was being mean. I would use the opportunity to say to her, "I'm not getting you lots of food because you don't need to be bigger than what you are now. You need to eat small meals to lose weight." Meanwhile, I was binging on food and being a hypocrite.

The Bully

One day the friend I called fat took us to a neighborhood close by and introduced us to her cousins and some friends who went to school on the other side of town. I was excited because she introduced me to her cousin's boyfriend at the time. He was cute and very charming. We exchanged numbers that night and sure enough, he called me. The only thing was, I did not have a cellphone, so I gave him our house phone number. I was excited but nervous at the same time. So, I coached him on the times he should call me. Then I started ditching my girlfriends after school and going straight home to wait on his phone calls. He called me every day after school. I would unplug the other phones in the house so my cousin or her husband wound not get on the phone and listen. After a week of ditching the girls, they noticed I was up to something and one of my girlfriends told me that he had a girlfriend and that I should leave him alone.

I said, "What are you talking about, he told me he likes me, and he doesn't have a girlfriend." So, I started avoiding her and pursuing him even more. And then it was official, within weeks we were boyfriend and girlfriend. I was so excited. He told me he loved me, he bought me things and gave me money to buy lunch at school. I thought I was so grown up because I had an official boyfriend. Even though I knew he was dating someone else, I did not care, it did not seem to bother me. He told me I was his girlfriend and that was all that mattered at the time. To make things even more official I took him to get our picture taken. We went to this place called Glamour Shots and they gave us lots of prints which we shared with our friends. That way I knew everyone was going to know we were for sure dating. We even matched, we both wore red. In one of the pictures he was kissing my cheek and I had my eyes closed. We were totally into each other. He lived within walking distance of my neighborhood. He got out of school earlier than I did so every day after school he would walk to my neighborhood and wait for my friends and me to get off the bus and we would go hang out until it was time for my friends and me to go home.

After everyone knew we were dating we all hung out together. He always came with his cousin, the friend I called fat liked him a lot, but he was not so much into her. She desperately craved his attention and I knew it. So, just like the bully I was, I would ask my boyfriend's cousin if he liked her and he would be honest and say, "Not like that." And I would use that to make fun of her. Every time the "fat" girl and I got into an argument I would say, "That's why so-and-so does not like you. Maybe if you did not have so many pimples, he would start looking at you." I used to tell her that she needed to get rid of her pizza face and lose weight, maybe he could like you boys like girls with nice bodies.

This boyfriend and I would hold hands and kiss in front of all our friends when we were hanging out and they just looked at us for some reason. I loved the attention I was getting, both from my boyfriend and the other girls. I used to think I had a boyfriend because I was prettier and curvier than they were, and it made me feel good about myself. At that point, I was sixteen and willingly having sex with my boyfriend and they knew it because I would come and tell them everything every time. I knew they were not yet sexually active, and they would ask me all these questions and was so excited to tell them. Telling them about something they were not yet participating in gave me a feeling of control and I loved it. I knew something they had no idea about—at least I thought so. I was the one with the boyfriend and the money, because not only did I do hair on the weekend and got paid, but my boyfriend was also giving me money. I was responsible for buying my friends food or something when we went somewhere, so I would always talk to them as if they were my children and not my friends.

I can honestly say that I loved my friends, but I treated them badly to make myself feel better. Only if I had known the Word of God, I would have known that I was carrying a load too heavy, that I wanted to distribute it to the closest people around me, my friends. Like the Word of God says in Matthew, "Take my yoke upon you, and learn of me; for I am meek and lowly in heart: and ye shall find rest unto your souls" (11:29). I was yearning for a place of rest mentally, and I would say I found some sort of happiness in making fun of others. I wish that I would have called on the LORD to give me rest. I now know that the LORD frees us from our heavy burdens. Jesus promises us love, healing, and peace when we devote our lives to the Word of God.

One day I was just so out of it that I decided that I was going to end my life and just be done with it. I thought that life was not worth living anymore. I went to the kitchen, took a knife out of the drawer, and ran out of the house. I was so sure I was going to kill myself there was no way around it. As I was running and thinking of a place to go, I ran into an apartment building and went down to the laundry room. It was quiet and dark, and I sat on the floor breathing heavily. Then I pointed the knife to my chest. As I pulled the tip of the knife closer to my heart, I heard a voice say, "If you try this not only will you not die, but it will be the greatest pain you have ever felt in your life." I was afraid because I had never heard such a voice speak to me before. I slowly put the knife down as I heard the siren. I sat there in silence until one of our neighbors ran through the door and saw me sitting there with the knife. He said to me, "Its ok, Saffie. Just put the knife down, it's not the end."

A policeman came in and wanted to take me to the hospital for an evaluation. I looked at him and said, "I am not crazy. I'm just tired of living in my body, can you help me come out of my body?" He looked at me and said, "I know you are not crazy. How about we go for a ride in my car, just to talk?" I agreed and went with him. He was a nice officer and he shared with me that he had teenagers and he understood that life gets tough, but he believed in me. He told me he believed that I could get through the tough times. We had a long, heartwarming conversation and he told me he still had to take me into the hospital, but he would let the doctors and nurses know what we had talked about. My cousin was so worried. She loves me and wants the best for me. Hearing that I wanted to take my own life was heartbreaking for her. I could see it on her face, but she understood and never judged me like most African family members would have. She embraced me. Even without me telling her, she knew that I was going through something. She did the best she could by being a mother figure to my sister and me.

I went to school the next day as if nothing had happened. Outside of the people in my house, only my neighbor knew. I kept it a secret just like all the other secrets I had been keeping locked up in my heart. I did not want my friends to think I was weird, or crazy. What would it sound like if I told them, "Hey guys, I wanted to kill myself yesterday, but a voice spoke to me and told me not to and I listened"? It sounded bizarre to me, so I was sure it would have sounded much worse to them.

I wondered quite a lot about the voice I had heard. Something in me was telling me it was God, but I told myself it could not have been. If it was God, then where was He when I was being exploited, being taken advantage of all my life? Where was He when I was robbed of my virginity? I continued to question, *who was that, and why does this voice even care to talk to me?* I wanted to know who that voice was.

But after all my curiosity about the voice, I somehow stopped questioning one day and never wondered about it again. I just wanted to put everything behind me as I had done with all the years past. All I wanted was a fresh start. I didn't want to allow my past to haunt me any longer. I tried the whole positive thinking thing. I thought, *If I just focus on me and how to get good grades in school and work hard, I will be fine, and I will be able to get into a great college and move away and start my life over.*

There were days I wanted out of my body for just a second, to take a break from it all. It was draining and unbearable at times. I had good days where I went about my day as a normal teenager, but most days were filled with confusion and tormenting flashbacks I could not avoid. Those were my worst days. Those days I look back on and refer to myself as the bully.

Twisted Love

Flee fornication. Every sin that a man doeth is without the body; but he that committeth fornication sinneth against his own body. What? Know ye not that your body is the temple of the Holy Ghost which is in you, which ye have of God, and ye are not your own? For ye are bought with a price: therefore glorify God in your body, and in your spirit, which are God's.

1 Corinthians 6:18-20

Before I accepted Jesus Christ as my LORD and personal Savior, I had no concept of sexual immorality. Yes, I was taught to save myself until marriage, but I had never heard of sexual immorality. And one might ask, "Is it not the same thing?" That was the same question I asked when I first heard of it at church. But I came to find there is more to sexual immorality than just saving yourself until marriage. And then there is this question: God created sex, and one of the purposes of sex is for our pleasure, right? Then why did He set limitations on the enjoyment of sex?

I learned that the limitations were set for our protection. When we stray outside the limitations, then we enter into sexual immorality. When I met the man who made my heart skip a beat every time I talked to him or saw him, I was living outside of the protective boundaries. You know, the kind of love where you never want to leave or hang up the phone, because when you did all you did was think of him? At seventeen years old I can say I didn't really understand love. I didn't even know what it meant to be quite honest. But I know how I felt. I was extremely happy with him. Outside of the love I felt with my father, this man-made me truly happy and it felt good to be happy again. I felt secure with him, I felt comforted by him, he became my place of safety. So, I clung to him like a child would cling to their parent. With bullying out of the way I found my place of happiness. My heart was uncontrollably drawn to him, unwaveringly hooked on him, and always filled to capacity with warmth every time I thought of him. I was obsessed with him. He became my drug of choice, swimming in sexual immorality. I can't lie; it felt good while it lasted. But I suffered the consequences later.

How We Met

One evening, I was walking home after attending an after-school activity and saw two gentlemen and one of my neighbors outside. They were just talking and hanging out it seemed. I thought nothing of it. I said hello to my neighbor and kept walking toward my building. But as I passed by them, I could feel their eyes on me every step of the way, so I quickened my pace. One of the guys got up and walked behind me. He noticed that my speed had increased and said, "If you don't stop, I am going to walk in the building with you." With fear, I stopped abruptly and turned around. He smiled and looked at me, "You live around here?" he asked. "As much as I come around here, I have never seen you." As he tried to make small talk, I just stood there and smiled at him. I finally told him my name. When he said he liked my name he noticed that I blushed and then he said, "Can we be friends?" I told him, "No," and then he asked for my phone number and I said, "No," again. He was persistent and did not take no for an answer, I turned around and reached for the entry door. He yelled behind me, "If you don't give me your number, I am going to walk in there with you as if you invited me into your house."

I thought to myself, *Oh no, you cannot walk in this house with me I'll get in trouble,* I was coming home late from a school activity and if he dared to walk into the house with me I'd be in big trouble. So out of fear, I gave him my number and ran in the house hoping he would never call me.

But as I was running in the house, I heard my phone ring. I started to reach for it but something told me not to, it was him calling trying to verify the number. I ignored it the first time, but he kept calling back to back so I finally answered and sure enough it was him. I picked up and said, "Hello." He said, "I was trying to make sure you did not give me a wrong number." I replied "It's me. Call me back later, I need to get settled."

That night he texted me and by my responses, he must have known I was starting to get annoyed at him so he told me goodnight and he would talk to me another time. He also told me it was nice meeting me and he wanted nothing from me but genuine friendship. As I was reading the message, I took a deep breath knowing he just wanted to be friends. I went to bed and woke up the next morning and saw that he had texted me that morning: "Good morning beautiful hope you have a great day at school today."

I rolled over and sat on the edge of the bed smiling as I read the message again and again. I did not reply immediately. I went into the restroom and sat on the commode and read it, again and again, smiling each time I read it. Sitting there, I realized I had wasted a lot of time reading the text message and did not have time to shower. So, I quickly brushed my teeth and washed my face and headed for my room to put my clothes on. Like a normal teenager, I took my time getting dressed because each day was a dress-to-impress day. Not this day, however. I grabbed the first thing I could reach in my closet and within minutes I ran out the door to catch the school bus. His text message had made my day. Even though I almost missed the bus that morning, I was so happy. I read and re-read the message the entire twenty-minute ride to school, but I still did not respond to it.

I felt a giddy, ecstatic high. This was before I knew anything about the neurotransmitter, dopamine, and the love hormone, oxytocin, that are elevated when someone is in love. It was the, "You are on drugs high." The feeling I got during this time of knowing him was as addictive as cocaine or any other powerful drug you could imagine. That text message was my gateway into it. I read it all day and when I got home that evening, he texted me again and said he hoped I had a great day at school and that he was thinking of me. I replied then, and we started texting back and forth until it was late into the night. Then he called and said, "I just wanted to hear your voice before we go to bed." He was saying all the right things at the right times. Initially, I just wanted to be friends like he had suggested but I was starting to really like him, just within days of meeting him. At the same time, I was not trying to rush things; I did not allow my feelings to push me. I wanted to keep things in perspective. If it was meant to be, only time would tell if what I was feeling, was in fact, love.

He would call me daily, and most mornings I woke up to his, "Good morning beautiful," text messages. It was a great way to start my day. I always looked forward to those morning texts. After weeks of talking on the phone, he finally asked me on a date. Not knowing what lie I was going to tell to get out of the house on a Friday night, I told him that I would let him know later if I could go out. Luckily, I was able to come up with something that afternoon and off we went on our first date. We went out to eat and then made our way to see a movie.

He had the traditional dating etiquette down to a T. He arrived on time as promised, gave me a hug when he saw me, and told me how delightful I looked. He turned the music down when I got into the car and wanted to talk, asking about my day and how it went. He was well dressed and smelled good. He always smelled luscious. (Yes, I said luscious.) I would always sniff him when I saw him, that's how good he smelled to me. He always opened doors, tried to pull out my chair this didn't always go well, supported me walking in my heels, and gave me genuine compliments. Besides, I could tell that he was just a good person, a considerate guy who knew the pleasure of treating a young lady as such. And the highlight of the night—he had a great sense of humor! He made me laugh throughout the evening, he was never corny but just incredibly funny.

After that first date, we went out every weekend. He would pick me up every Friday night, the only night I could get away going out, lying and claiming I had extracurricular activities for school. Most of the time we went out to eat then to the movies. For a time, we saw every newly released movie out there, and no matter what was going on with his busy work schedule we always went out on Friday nights. Knowing I could depend on him to show up for me after working full time every single day was a great feeling.

Consistency does speak for itself. Knowing he was there for me made me feel loved and special. Since he was so consistent, I knew he was committed. I had no worries because he was too busy actually doing everything he promised and that was refreshing to me. Yes, he was not perfect, but I noticed all the little things he was consistent with and that made our relationship extra special. Like how he always texted me each morning and how he wanted to hang out with me every Friday night. The way he hugged me and kissed my forehead when he saw me even when I was mad at him at times. Little things that would often go unnoticed, but since I was high on love, and considering my past, I noticed it all and it made me feel extra special.

Fighting for Love

One night, at about midnight I received an inmate call from Fairfax County Jail. It was him. I was hesitant to answer my phone at first since I did not recognize the number. After a couple of missed calls, I finally picked up and it was him on the phone. "You would not believe what happened to us," he said to me as I answered the phone. "What in the world happened? What are you doing in there?" I asked him. He explained to me that my ex-boyfriend and his friends tried to jump him at a house party. He had invited me to the party, but I couldn't go due to the time, it was late into the night and I was not allowed to stay out, so he went with his friends. Apparently, my ex-boyfriend was trying to get back with me when he found out I was dating someone new. When we broke up, I thought we both had shipped each other off to an imaginary island where we were free to roam around and drink as many coconut juices as possible. Apparently, he felt a bit different about the whole thing and he started creeping back to the city when he heard I was dating someone new.

So, one of my ex's friends was in the hospital and my boyfriend and one of his friends were in jail and I was in shock and crying. I kept saying, "OMG! OMG!" Underneath it all, my mind was working about a thousand miles an hour wondering, *How do we even go about getting you both out of there?* I then said out loud through my tears, "I've never bailed someone out of jail. I don't even know where to start." He quickly said, "I will call my mother and have you meet up with her first thing Monday morning."

Since she lived in Maryland and I lived in Virginia, he gave me his mother's phone number to arrange our meeting. He got locked up over the weekend, so he had to wait until Monday, a business day, to be bailed out. He was so worried that I cried even harder. I felt so bad that he was in jail and that the situation had also landed a person in the hospital. I also felt bad not knowing how this was all going to unwind.

I went to bed that night worried. I turned and tossed the whole night. The next morning, I took it upon myself to call the guy who was in the hospital to check on him and see how he was doing. I was told I could not talk with him and should wait until he was discharged. That made me even more worried. At that point, they had told him he could press charges. I called some of our mutual friends and told them what had happened. They said they would try to convince him not to press charges. But we found out his parents were really upset and wanted him to press charges. We had to wait, we could not do anything until Monday morning anyway.

Monday came and I talked to my future mother-in-law. She told me she was on her way to the courthouse along with the mother of his friend. Since I did not drive or own a car they came and picked me up. Somehow both mothers were on top of the game and told me they each had found lawyers who were meeting up with us to look at the case and to arrange bail if possible. The ride to the courthouse was the most awkward, stretched-out moment ever. It was my first time meeting his mother. It certainly wasn't the way I had imagined meeting my future mother-in-law. The first meeting, or so I had thought and hoped, usually takes place within months of courting, long before walking down the aisle, and generally, never on the way to a courthouse to get your future husband out of jail. This was just the beginning of the big roller coaster ride.

We met with both lawyers and they told us the charges were not looking good. They also said they could bail them out, but they needed a hefty fee of a couple of thousand dollars. Of course, to me, two thousand dollars was a lot of money, but the two moms took it in stride and didn't blink an eye. They agreed, made the payment, and the attorneys assured them their sons would be bailed out.

This was my first time ever going to a courthouse. The lawyer walked us into a room where we were able to see my boyfriend and his friend on a monitor as the judge told them the charges against them and their bail amount. As we sat there waiting for them to be called, we noticed there were a lot of people in court that day for fighting and many other crimes. This was all new to me. I felt out of place; I did not want to be there at all. Being there made me nauseous.

They were finally called, separately, and when we saw them, they did not look like themselves. I immediately started crying when I saw my boyfriend on the monitor as the judge was talking to him. I could feel his mother looking at me as I was crying. She wasn't happy either, but I could tell she wanted to say something to me. While we were sitting in that room, she did not say anything to me. We left after we saw them and waited for the lawyer to give us his final word before we headed home. About an hour later the lawyer called and said they were both going to be bailed out the following day. Thankfully, they only spent a couple of days in jail. The boy who was injured did not press charges and the case was dropped a couple of weeks later.

The Shock of My Life

Just as we were walking out of the room and heading for the elevator his mother looked at me and said, "I hope you know he has a baby on the way. He has a pregnant girlfriend at home as we speak."

My mouth and face dropped to the floor. I was speechless. I just stood there and stared at the wall in shock. I just froze in silence, my mouth opened slightly, and started shaking like I was trying to say something but could not find the words. I thought to myself, *What in the world just happened?* It was like I had just heard the most horrific thing of my life. She saw that I was obviously in shock and didn't know how to respond. She then said, "I can see you he did not tell you, but I am telling you now. You seem like a very nice young lady, please just leave him alone. He has a baby on the way with his girlfriend. I am sure you can find a nice guy out there for yourself Leave him alone.

I did not say a word, and she was not expecting me to. I heard everything she said, and she started walking toward the parking lot and I followed. I was hoping at this point that I had another way home, but I did not, so I had to ride with both mothers in my shocked and turned-upside-down state of mind.

They dropped me off and I went home and collapsed in my bed and took a nap straight away. It was all too much to think about. When I woke up in the middle of the night I sat on my bed and began to wonder, *How, is that I can never really find true happiness?* Every time I began to think about all the things, I have encountered I started crying and then wondered, *What is it? Am I even normal? Why is it I always have something to battle with even when I try to forget about the past somehow?*

I always found myself in troubling and very painful situations. *Why is this happening to me? Do I even deserve true happiness? Maybe*

I was born to endure pain forever. I know being in any sort of pain is uncomfortable, even the most trivial pain is uncomfortable, such as a cut or a stubbed toe. But that kind of pain is certain to subside within a short period of time. But when I imagine my pain it's the kind of pain that is serious, the kind that never seems to fade away, and this kind of chronic mental pain was starting to have a negative impact on me emotionally. Any kind of chronic pain is certain to have a negative effect on a person and I was definitely negatively affected. But one thing I knew for sure: I felt loved with this guy and I was not about to let that go. With him, I felt safe, he was my safe haven. Why should I let him go?

So, I made up my mind that even with all I knew, at that point I still was not going to give him up. Of course, I brought it up to him and he did what every man out there would do: He minimized it and I fell for it and believed him. But I wanted to believe him, deep inside I knew he was minimizing the situation and painting a less tragic image for me and that worked since that's what I wanted anyway. I know many people may hate to hear this but it's true, you know when someone is lying to you and you decide if you want to turn a deaf ear to the truth and believe the lies. I knew, but I turned a deaf ear to it. With him I did not feel pain—he was my drug of choice. I did what I had to do, I took the drug that was working for my pain and the relationship continued.

Word got out, everyone found out I was dating some guy from Maryland and he had a baby on the way. People hated me for that. I still did not give in, I didn't care. All I knew was that he told me they were not in a relationship and they were only having a baby together and that was enough for me not to care.

Months went by, and one day I was complaining that I needed to get my hair done and had no one to do it. He offered that his pregnant girlfriend knew how to do hair and if I wanted her to do it, she would. Without hesitating I said okay. He set it up and I was picked up and taken to the house. When I entered, she took a great x-ray look at me and said, "Nice to meet you," in her very so pregnant state. I sat down and started eating and drinking food he had bought on our way to the house. I accidentally spilled my drink and he looked at her and told her to clean it up. At that point, I got up quickly and said, "No I will clean it up. She is pregnant and she can't do that kind of stuff with her big belly."

He went upstairs and minutes later he called me, and I went to him. Writing this makes me cry. When I went upstairs, we had sex in their bed while she was downstairs. Looking back at our actions, she could have killed us both and I am sure she could have pled "not guilty" and gotten off scot-free. We had sex on their bed, and she knew. This was the first of many episodes of this selfish act. I washed up and told him I did not want my hair done anymore and I wanted to go home. When we came downstairs I could see the sadness on her face. I felt bad for a minute or two and then I walked out the door. Talk about sexual immorality...it doesn't get any worse than that. Pain can make you do anything to feel better; what you do to cure your pain, however, should never be at the cost of others' happiness. And here I was doing just that. I did not care at all. If it made me feel good, I did it.

When their baby was born it was the perfect time for me to just walk away and let them be. But I didn't. I couldn't do that. When his child was born, he told me all about it and kept me involved in the process. Weeks into being a new parent I could tell he really wanted to be a great father to his daughter, and I could also see that he was trying to push back from me. I noticed it and I did not give him a chance to. When he would not call or text me, I filled his phone up with all sorts of messages telling him how much he meant to me and how much I loved him. I worked overtime to keep his attention and he fell for it.

The relationship continued and I never relaxed trying to show how I respected him and how I wanted to do whatever he wanted. I knew one thing he loved, and I gave him a full dose of it. He liked seeing me dressed up and going out with him, and I did just that. I was fun and spontaneous and when he wanted to have sex, I was available. We had sex everywhere: in their house, on their bed, in the car, on the kitchen counter, in the living room, in the closet, in parking lots, outside. Everywhere and anywhere we could think of and had access to. We loved it and we did not care, it felt great. We loved each other in a very twisted way. Yes, we had a very intimate relationship, but we were also genuine friends. I cared about him and he cared about me. We found ourselves in a very strange kind of love.

I loved him, and I disregarded the fact that he lied to me. The whole time I was dating him he was in a relationship and had a baby on the way. When the baby was born I decided to continue the relationship despite what I knew. We both played a part in dwelling in sexual sin, and we enjoyed living in it. God created sex to be a beautiful and essential ingredient of marriage, but sex outside of marriage will always end up hurting someone. And most importantly, we hurt God when we follow our own desires instead of the Word of God.

We violated the commitment necessary for him to be a good father to his baby and a good boyfriend to his baby's mother. Never play a part in another person's pain during the process of finding your own happiness. I was so desperate to find happiness when I was presented with something, I clung to it despite the consequences. I know you have heard the saying, "Hurting people hurt people," and that is exactly what the situation was. I was hurt and did not mind hurting others. I had no remorse about what I was doing at the time; I had an "I-don't-care" attitude about it all. Sometimes I would even say, "Oh well, it's not my fault he wants to be with me." I simply turned a deaf ear to it all.

I did not care about anything people told me about him. All I knew was he was my boyfriend and nothing else mattered. Imposing pain on others is simply a symptom of one's own overflowing pain. We all have a threshold of pain, and the breaking point is when the dam of self-control breaks and the pain floods out. Unfortunately, my pain flooded onto a relationship and I closed myself off from any feelings of guilt or shame.

Girl Talk 101: Do not ignore the facts, I know it feels good to relieve your pain but it's only temporary. Genuine happiness can only come from a true and honest relationship. You are too precious to be a side piece. Sexual sin is a sin against your own body, the only sin that is against your body. Your body is a temple and you should always respect the temple.

To Hold or Not

"For I know the thoughts that I think toward you," saith the LORD, "thoughts of peace, and not of evil, to give you an expected end."

Jeremiah 29:11

Three years later, I was still dating him. At twenty years old I became pregnant with his child. Now what? I was pregnant and did not know what I was going to do. I thought I was so invincible that getting pregnant was just not possible. At first, I took measures to protect myself against disease and pregnancy but somewhere along the way I lost my senses as I floated on that incredible high. Even though I was pregnant and about to have a child in that oh-so-dysfunctional relationship I enjoyed myself anyway. When I started experiencing the pregnancy symptoms I was confused. I knew something was off with my body and I tried to blame it on everything and anything else I could think of.

After a couple of weeks of denial, I finally decided I was going to take the test; at least the pregnancy test from the drug store would confirm it. So one day soon after, I drove to the drug store and bought a test kit. At that point, I had a little rundown car I was driving from point A to point B. It was just good enough, I felt, for short trips. It looked terrible, and it sounded just as bad, but I loved that car. It was my car and it gave me a huge sense of independence. I did not need him to take me everywhere anymore, I drove myself places. And it was perfect. I did not tell him. I went and got the test on my own and went home. I was so nervous I thought of doing the test at the drugstore but changed my mind halfway into the restroom. I reversed and ran out of the drug store and got into my car and zoomed home as fast as I could.

Despite my old-grandma driving style, I think I am a pretty good driver because I went to an actual driving school. I was so eager to drive when I was younger and wanted to do this one thing the right way for once. I still consider learning to drive one of my greatest achievements.

I had been looking at pregnancy tests online all week and knew I had to be able to pee on the stick. I had been drinking plenty of water that day and was prepared to empty my bladder. *This is the moment of truth,* I thought to myself. For some reason, as soon as I had parked the car everything started moving in slow motion. I got out of the car, slowly entered the house, went straight up the stairs, and walked into the restroom. I stared at the toilet for what seemed to be an eternity, then I saw myself opening the test packaging. Half of me wanted to just throw it away and run out of there as fast as I could and go to bed to hide from the inevitable. I knew what the test was going to show, but I wanted to distance myself from reality as much as possible and pretend that I really wasn't in the dilemma I was experiencing.

I suddenly realized there was no escape from the present or the future for that matter, and so I peed on the stick and voila! I saw the two faded pink lines appear and they turned darker and darker. Pregnancy was confirmed, there was a baby inside me. *What in the world just happened?* I thought. I was stunned by the news, but I knew right away I wanted to keep the baby. I looked down at my stomach and placed both hands on it. I wanted to feel something. I had my hands on my stomach for quite a while until I realized I could not feel anything but the rising and falling of my heavy breathing. I was in the bathroom for a good half-hour just looking at my stomach in the mirror, hoping to feel or see some physical confirmation of the pregnancy.

Of course, I did not feel or see anything, I wasn't far enough along yet. Now I had to get rid of the packaging quickly so nobody would figure out I was pregnant. I cut the packaging into little pieces and took the trash out to my car. There was no way I was going to leave any evidence in the house. I drove all the way to a public place and stuffed it in a trash can.

I could not stop thinking, *I am going to be a mother.* Thinking about being a mother was exciting. I wanted to be happy about being a mother. I remember suddenly feeling excited. I drove home from the trash can full of joy. The excitement I felt came from within. I went home and did the usual—ate and went into my room to do my class assignment. Through my madness I always loved school. Getting good grades made me happy and nothing was going to stop that. So, I went and did my homework as usual.

At that time, I was attending the local community college after getting my Practical Nursing License (LPN). I was working as an LPN on the weekends and going to school during the week pursuing my degree as a Registered Nurse. I was just finishing my prerequisite to get into the RN program, which I had applied to. I was just awaiting my acceptance letter. I knew I was going to get in due to my good grades and being an LPN I had an even greater chance of being accepted into the program, so I was not worried. The same week I found out I was pregnant was the week I received my acceptance letter into the Registered Nurse Program at Northern Virginia Community College. Now I had two big, exciting pieces of news to celebrate. But all on my own—I did not tell him I was pregnant or about my acceptance into the RN program. I was so happy, but I was afraid his response would be negative, so I kept it to myself, at least for a few weeks. I did not want my joy to fade away.

I was looking forward to these exciting moments of my life. With a baby on the way and pursuing my nursing degree, I knew my life was about to change completely. A couple of weeks into my joy I decided to tell him one morning; I knew it was time to spill the beans. I went into the slow-motion act again. I dialed his number on my phone, even though his number was already on speed dial I felt the need to type it in at that moment. As usual, he answered and did his usual thing: "Good morning beautiful, how did you sleep?" And on and on he went as if life never changed. I stopped him and said, "I have to tell you something important. I took a test and it says I am pregnant."

"Wow, you are?"

And I replied, "Yes I am. I took the test already." He then asked me, "What do you want to do Saffie?" Without any hesitation, I said, "I want to keep it." He responded and said, "I am with you, we will do whatever you want to do."

I felt myself exhaling slowly as if I had been holding my breath as he finished the sentence. I was relieved. I told him I was going to call him right back and rushed off the phone. Whew, one hill knocked down and now I had to tell my family and friends.

That same week I told my family the news, and they were also very supportive and wanted me to go on with the pregnancy. Then I told a very few of my friends, most were happy and worried at the same time, knowing the situation with my unborn baby's father. But ultimately, they were all very supportive. So now everyone on my priority list knew I was happy and looking forward to being a mother. Instantly, when it was confirmed by testing from the physician, I felt an even deeper joy, an unexplainable happiness that can never be compared to anything in the world. However, I knew this experience came with a responsibly that could sometimes be overwhelming, especially for someone like me, a young lady in a very complicated relationship. I had to mentally prepare myself to be a single mother. I did not know the decisions he was going to make, and I couldn't even begin to guess. At this point, his daughter was about three years old and was still with her mother and he was still dating me, that much I knew. I was not expecting him to leave her, but I wondered quite a bit about how it was all going to turn out once his baby mother found out about my pregnancy. We never really discussed it, but we knew she was going to find out somehow.

I blocked that part of my reality out and figured I had to focus on me and the growing baby in my belly, making sure I was taking my prenatal vitamins daily and reading up on foods and activities I should stay away from. I was so intrigued, I was reading up on the different trimesters and what to expect, and signs and symptoms to report to my doctor. I was all in. I even download an app that updated me weekly on how far along my baby was growing, and how the baby would be developing week-by-week. I was making sure I did all the right things because more than anything, I wanted a healthy baby. Because I took care of sick kids, I knew how overwhelming it was to care for a sick child. Not to say all sick children are a result of what their mothers did not do right during pregnancy, but I wanted to at least do what was recommended. I withdrew from hanging out with friends or going to social gatherings because I did not want people to know I was pregnant. I was hiding, I only went to work, school, and church.

At this point, I had given my life to God. A friend invited me to church and I had started going occasionally until one day, I had an encounter I will never forget. The day I surrendered my life to Christ, I accepted Him as my LORD and personal Savior. What better timing to have given my life to God, because I was soon in for a rude awakening. I came to know God right before I found out I was pregnant. Yes, I know I was one of those Christians who was saved and still fornicating. I did not listen. We live and learn, right? I hope as you read this story it helps you see that it's much better to be obedient to the Word of God than not. I was not and I paid the consequences. However, my baby is a blessing and is one of the greatest gifts God has blessed me with. Later in life, I would reap what I had sown. There are consequences for sin.

Once everyone knew I was pregnant, the baby mother also found out. I'm not sure how she found out, but it was not a good show for either of us. All hell broke loose. It's one thing to know your man is cheating but it's a whole different ball game when you hear he's gotten someone pregnant. At the time, I did not care if she found out, I was preparing myself for my child and getting ready for my life to completely change, with or with the father of my child. I was focused on "doing me". He was stressed out about it all, of course, and was caught in the middle of two women. I know for a fact he loved her too. He was caught in the middle of love and did not know what to do.

He never talked to me about it, but I could always see it on his face—he was stressed out. She was also stressed out and hurt by the news. It was too painful to bear, so they broke up. He moved out and we moved in together. We thought we were going to move in together and live a happy life. Finally, with the baby mother out of the picture, now we could focus on us, our relationship, our baby and the whole parenthood thing. So, I thought, anyway—wishful thinking. Like any relationship, things were really good at the beginning. We read parenting books together and went to doctor's appointments together. We were both going to school, working, and just doing the best we could to prepare for what was ahead for us.

Then one day, I was called in to the doctor's office first thing in the morning to come in for my test results. Screening for certain diseases or conditions is offered as a routine part of prenatal care for all pregnant women, regardless of age. But since I was young, I just knew I would have no issues as long as I was doing the right things during my pregnancy. Still, in my first trimester, we did a blood test to confirm the pregnancy and to detect any abnormalities with the growing fetus. The results were in and the doctor called us to come into his office to explain the findings. Straight away, being in the medical field I knew whenever you receive a call from your doctor after testing to come in for your results means there were abnormal findings. My heart started quivering, I could feel it just beating. We both looked at each other and I burst into tears. I was devastated, he looked at me and said, "Don't worry Saffie, no matter what happens I promise you that I will always be here with you." He just held me in his arms. He knew I needed him more than ever now.

All sorts of crazy thoughts were running through my head as we got ready and headed to the doctor's office that morning. We got there and the nurse, who was not professional at all, came out and began reading the findings to us in the office waiting room. We both got upset and asked the nurse to please take us in a private room and explain to the results to us privately. She rolled her eyes and said, "Ok, follow me." I finally said, "Please get the doctor in here. I do not want to talk with you, I prefer the doctor himself." She went and called him in. He could feel the tension in the room and apologized straight away before we could even explain. He went over the results and said, "There is a great chance that the baby will have Down Syndrome."

I looked at him and said, "What? Please repeat that again because I do not think I heard you correctly." Then he repeated the statement again: "There is a great chance that the baby will have Down Syndrome." I remember closing my eyes at that moment and thinking to myself, *That's it, God hates me. He hates me so much that He can't even allow me to enjoy this moment.* I wanted to cry but I told myself, *No, I will no longer cry because of my pain. I began questioning God again. If You knew you were going to bring me into this world to just suffer one thing after the other, then why did You even create me?* At this point in my life, I was reading my Bible and studying the Word of God. I knew that God had created me and He also said He knew me before I was formed in my mother's womb. (See Jeremiah 1:5.) So I asked Him, *Then why have I suffered so much at such a young age?* I knew at twenty years old, most girls my age were just starting to understand who they were and finding their place in society. But for me, it was much more than that. I felt like I had the pain of the world stuffed inside me and I kept experiencing one painful thing after another.

I was angry at God. Were these the thoughts He had for me as stated in the book of Jeremiah, "'For I know the thoughts that I think toward you,' saith the LORD, 'thoughts of peace, and not of evil, to give you an expected end'" (29:11). Up to this point in my life, nothing was of peace. All I knew and had experienced was pain and confusion, so what are His thoughts for me then? I screamed out loud. *Does this not apply to me because I am a sinner and not living a Godly life?* All these questions were racing in my head.

The doctor stood there in silence allowing me to vent and have my rant. He then said, "This is just the first step of the screening, we have to do more testing to confirm the results." I was a little relieved to know this was not the confirmation results. He gave information on where to go for the testing and we went home. We were so emotionally beaten down that we both went home and went straight to bed. It was such an exhausting day. We were not ready to share the news with anyone, so we kept it to ourselves. After a long nap that morning, we woke up and began searching the internet for similar situations. There were lots of stories of misleading findings, but also ones that turned out to be true. With more frustration and confusion, I picked up the Bible and went straight to the book of Jeremiah again. Even though I was angry at God I knew I could find some comforting words in the Bible, at least enough to get through the day. The Word of God became my source of comfort. I could not stop thinking about the verse in Jeremiah that says he knew Jeremiah before he formed him in his mother's womb and had sent him apart to be a prophet of the nations. Now here I was, asking God, "You, know my child before you formed him in my belly, did you really form him to be a Down Syndrome child?" Not to say anything bad of people with Down Syndrome, honestly, the sweetest people I have ever come across are people with Down Syndrome. But something inside me could not accept this diagnosis. I knew this was not the end of the story. With all my anger and questions, I knew this was not it. We called and scheduled the appointment as recommended, but we had to wait a couple of weeks for the first available date.

So there was nothing we could do but to wait. While waiting, we began praying and believing that our child did not have Down Syndrome. Our faith was so deep, we just knew he did not have it and we kept praying and believing the test would confirm that. After praying for some time, I decided to share the news with a couple of my family members and church family and they were all praying with us, believing that the test would tell us the baby did not have Down Syndrome. It's great to pray by yourself but sometimes you just need a couple of believers to believe and pray with you. This made a great difference, people calling and praying with us daily—we knew we were not alone. There was this particular sister who was with me through the whole thing. She prayed with me like she was praying for herself, she was so involved in the process. She called me daily, and sometimes she came over to spend time with me because she knew I was in distress and needed comforting. I thank God for her to this day for being by my side at such a difficult time in my life. Outside of my boyfriend, she was the closest person to me, and I truly needed her.

We waited and waited, and the time was approaching for the testing. A week before the testing my boyfriend had a court date for a fight he was involved in some years ago. He got the letter and I was thinking to myself, *What now LORD?* Just when I thought life could not get any worse. It was during this time when I found out to never say, "It cannot get any worse." Because it sure did for me. The day before the confirmation testing, we went to court. This was a real trial with a jury and everything. I thought it was just a little fight, as he explained to me, but when we got to the courtroom, I was terrified and could not sit in the room during the trial. It was just too much to handle.

The trial went on for two full days. On our drive home the first night we somehow got lost and a drive that was supposed to be a forty-five-minute ride took two hours. But we both knew it was a way for us to enjoy the time we had left with each other. We got home and were exhausted, so we both went to bed. He woke up in the middle of the night and kept saying he couldn't sleep, he wanted to just talk. Another sign. So I woke up and talked with him for as long as I could. The next morning, as we were getting ready to head out for the second day of court, he decided I should stay home. I listened and stayed home. He kissed me goodbye, gave me the tightest hug I could ever imagine, and he said he loved me and the baby. He kept me updated the entire time, then a couple of hours went by and I hadn't heard from him or anyone who was there with him. I was getting worried. Then the call came in, he was found guilty and was taken into custody.

I was not able to touch him or kiss him for the next eighteen months. He was found guilty and was incarcerated. He called me that night when he got into the detention center, very sad and disappointed. Nobody saw that coming.

Now, with the boyfriend gone, and a confirmation test to see if our baby had Down syndrome the following week, I could not even cry. I had no tears. I knew I had to be strong. He was heartbroken and depressed in jail and not knowing the results of the test made it even worse. I had no choice but to toughen up. He was my confidante. He was one person who brought me happiness and he was taken away from me. I thought this was the LORD punishing me for my sins. I was aching with grief: I had lost my friend, my lover, and the father of my growing baby. I struggled with anger towards God. There was nothing anyone could do to console me. Where was the LORD, the LORD of boundless mercy, of sovereignty and grace beyond my imagination? I felt He was very far from me, He was nowhere near me.

In the midst of my pain, I was reminded of Joseph's story. His brothers hurled him into a well and sold him into slavery, and God raised him up beside Pharaoh and saved his people. I then recognized that my suffering was not a punishment at all, but rather an action to bring about some tremendous good. Of course, this sounded good, but I remember saying, "Look, just make it stop, take away the pain." I knew God had the infinite capacity to affect happiness in our iniquity, His love for us was made perfect in the death and resurrection of His Son, Jesus Christ. The LORD had granted suffering in order to save me. But why was I suffering?

The days went by. My best friend was gone. So, the night before the confirmation test, I asked my sister in the LORD to come with me, in fact, she wanted to come with me, so it worked out perfectly. She came over and we prayed that night and continued praying into the morning, still believing the results would be good news. I was hopeful, and one thing I knew was that the Word of God gave me hope. In spite of my anger and questions, I still had hope. It was the moment of truth. We were ready for the great news, we took off and went to the appointment.

We arrived at the doctor's office and spent some time in the parking lot praying. My sister in the LORD was what I would consider a righteous Christian. At the time, I was still living in sin, fornicating and all. We went into the building and signed in, and in the waiting room we meet a Christian man who was so full of positive energy it was contagious. I was sitting quietly and just waiting to be called. As I sat there, I wondered with all these stressors around me, would I ever be able to hold my child in my arms? Would I ever be able to hold this baby? Staring out into space, I heard my name called. My heart was racing. The examiner noticed how stiff I was and told me to relax, that everything was going to work out in my favor. I looked at her and smiled and said, "Thank you, I just want to hear great news for once." She told me she was hoping for great news for me as well.

She started the test and I lay there, quiet and still. A couple of minutes went by and she did not say anything. Then I noticed she was smiling, and her face was lighting up. I stopped looking at the screen and was just looking at her facial reactions and fed off that—when she smiled, I smiled, when her face was serious, I got serious. And then boom! She confirmed all her findings were within normal ranges. I was so happy I lay back on the bed and let the tears flow. I was filled with joy all over again. We thanked God over and over again.

It was very important to me to thank the LORD for the victory. We often talk about the victory and the success and how God made a way, but we often stray from talking much about what to do after the victory. We must give thanks to the LORD. One important lesson you can learn in order to protect yourself from the devil's schemes and continue to stand strong in the LORD after the victory is to give thanks unto the LORD.

Professional Failure F++

And the LORD shall make thee the head, and not the tail; and thou shalt be above only, and thou shalt not be beneath; if that thou hearken unto the commandments of the LORD thy God, which I command thee this day, to observe and to do them.

Deuteronomy 28:13

At one point or another, everyone fails in life. This is just one of the realities we experience. You suffer through failure. We associate failure with total defeat. I can say this, because I have failed, repeatedly. At one point, I considered myself a professional failure because I kept failing repeatedly. I lived with a sense of total defeat. Nobody wants to fail, but all must fail in order to succeed. In fact, the most famous and influential people today have failed more times than the average person.

There is importance in failing, it has taught me some important lessons. When you fail, you learn, you mature, you grow, and you gain new understanding and perspective on life itself. Yes, failure hurts, but it is part of life. When you are going through pain, emotional or physical, you might not understand its usefulness at the moment. And when you are going through failure, it can hurt just as bad. In fact, if you have failed continuously like I have, the pain runs so deep you begin to question your very existence.

Questioning God was one of my favorite things to do. *Why this? Why me? Why do you hate me so much, God?* You name it and I asked it. I never saw the light everyone talks about—the one at the end of the tunnel. I just felt like I lived in that dark tunnel and would never move forward to see anything at its end. But I guarantee you, there is a light at the end of the tunnel, but you can only see that light when you continue to move towards it. I was living in the tunnel instead of moving toward the end of it, where the light was.

Eventually, failure taught me to never ever give up on my goals and dreams. Never ever give up on what God has put inside of you. You must become what God has created you to be. That's what I mean by moving forward and moving toward the light.

Over time, my countless failures brought me to a place where I could see clearly how they had shaped me for the better. Some of the lessons you learn through your failures are the most vital lessons you may ever learn in life. When I was going through my failures, I thought it was the end of the world. I was failing repeatedly, one class after the other. And when I failed, I failed big, and it felt like the end of the world. I felt like everything I ever dreamed of achieving was out of reach and would be for eternity. It was a feeling of tremendous hopelessness. Failure can take a toll on you. It broke me mentally, spiritually, and physically.

The summer of 2011 was a life-changing summer I will never forget. My boyfriend was in jail, I found out I was pregnant, I was told I was going to have a child with Down Syndrome—but by the grace of God, it was confirmed that the growing baby was fine.

Slowing but surely autumn came, and it was time for me to start the nursing program. Knowing how challenging nursing was going to be, I had to prepare for another life-changing experience. Fortunately, I worked my butt off that summer trying to save up as much as I could so when fall classes started, I would not have to work as much. That left more time to study and focus on passing my classes. However, with so much going on in my life it was almost impossible to focus. But I knew I wanted to become a registered nurse. Nursing has always been my passion, and I wanted to continue my education, so I just jumped in and forced myself to concentrate on succeeding.

The fall semester came, and classes started. I had a great friend who I met through taking the prerequisites course and we became sisters instantly. She was very supportive, and we studied together all the time. That was very much needed at that point in my life. Surround yourself with true friends. True friends inspire and motivate you. She was always there to uplift me, she believed in me even when I did not believe in me. She had no idea what I was going through, but I knew she could tell there was something different about me, despite the fact I had not mentioned anything to her yet. She was there for me when I needed her the most. She said positive things to uplift my spirit when I was down and never focused on the negative. During a couple of our first exams and assignments, she could tell I was not performing well. I was struggling in all my classes.

The very first semester in nursing school, I showed up, did the work, and tried my best by spending time studying but I was still not getting passing grades. I was barely making it. I even tried signing up for a tutor. I did all I could do to be successful in my classes, but I was still struggling. I would spend so much time studying for my exams but when the day of the exam came, I was so anxious I just could not focus on the exams. I was failing one exam after the other. I was hiding my pregnancy, I did not want people to know I was pregnant. I was hiding so much so that sometimes I forgot I was pregnant myself. I was so confused and worried and frustrated I had constant headaches and was constantly moody.

Slowly but surely my belly got bigger and bigger as the weeks went by and I started to gain weight, so I decided to tell my friend. I was a bit hesitant because I did not want to disappoint her or look bad in her eyes. We always talked about the future, finishing nursing school and working in the hospital and advancing our educations when we were done. Here I was pregnant, not passing my classes, and I knew telling might disappoint her because it was nothing like the conversations we normally had about the future. I knew she cared about me and my future, and despite the path I took she was there for me. She was indeed a true friend.

So often we see failure act as a friend filter; that is, when failures hit us, most friends leave. They only want to be around us when we are following the paths we had all planned and dreamed about. I was fortunate that she loved me and did not care if I was a failure. When you fail you might have friends and family members walk out on you, and it will feel as if everyone is betraying you. Just pay attention to their actions towards you and remember to let it be like a filter—a friend filter. The good ones will stay. Let the others go their own way.

The first semester was coming to an end and I had managed to pass at least two classes but was still failing my core classes. My emotions were all over the place and I did not know how to cope. With all the chaos, it was hard to stay focused. I was an emotional wreck, I felt as if I was going up and down like a roller-coaster ride. Failure is indeed painful, and very emotional. Too often I felt it was too much to bear. But I learned it was very important to be able to cope with my emotions. I knew I was going to fail at least one or two classes, so I had to just accept the facts as they were. I learned to refocus my mind and my thoughts on the positive things. Like the fact that the baby was growing and healthy with no complications for either of us. It was a blessing to realize that and I began thanking God for the good things I had in my life.

I came up with a new way to train my mind to think positively. Yes, I had lots of negative things that were happening, but at the same time, I had positive things happening too. My mind could not focus on the good things at first, but I had to adjust my mind's lens to focus just on the positive rather than the negative. Failure taught me how to cope with my emotions by simply refocusing on the positive. I had a lot to be thankful for. I was healthy enough to be able to work and go to school during my pregnancy and I had a loving and supportive family. My friends were also very understanding and supportive.

My main support system, however, was my relationship with the LORD. I had just given my life to Christ as my LORD and Savior. If I had only known what it really meant to be saved at that time, I could have seen things a lot differently. But I know it happened the way it did for a reason, and I can honestly say my many failures have shaped my life to be who I am becoming today. As a baby Christian, it is vital to understand what it means to be saved. I was saved but still living a lost life. I was lost and confused. I prayed, I believed in God, and I knew He was in charge of my life. But I did not quite understand that being saved meant I needed to completely turn away from a life without God. You know the whole ordeal of giving up our wants, pleasures, importance, and the most difficult one—our power. I thought that if I studied harder and longer, I could succeed.

I don't mean to degrade academics, but I needed more than just studying. I needed to know it was not by my power but only by His that success, if any at all, came into my life. When God became part of my life, I did not realize the focus on myself alone had no future and offered nothing of real, lasting value. But I wanted to be a nurse so I could take care of the ill, thinking I was going to advance the great cause of humanity through healing and medicine. Not knowing for sure if I wanted to be part of such advancement, I really needed to be saved from myself. I needed to live a life focused on the will of God and living this faith daily, knowing His will is far greater than my own. I always wanted something out of life—I wanted the pain to go away, I wanted the man, I wanted the degree, I wanted the baby. I wanted, wanted, wanted...I just wanted to accumulate, and such a pattern came from my need to fill a void in my life. What I really needed was a life of healing and wholeness. I was longing for love and belonging.

The semester came to an end and I had failed the most important class of the first semester. I was sad, angry, and frustrated, but mostly ashamed of the fact that I failed. I was not going to be able to graduate with my friend as we had planned. Nursing school classes are only offered during certain semesters and they could not be taken during summer school. So here I was, going to graduate a year later now, and that was only if I passed all the other courses in the following semesters. I knew there was nothing I could do on my end, so I just accepted it. I was a failure. It was very difficult knowing I was not going to graduate on time.

Sometimes we set these timelines for ourselves as if we are God and are in full control of our lives. What I failed to realize was that God is the One in control of it all. I had my life all planned out: at a certain age I was going to be graduating from college with a nursing degree, then I would get a great job, get married, buy the single-family home with the white picket fence, have the beautiful children, and live happily ever after. Then, of course, reality set in and I found myself in totally different circumstances. I was not going to graduate from nursing school on time, I was not married but pregnant, and the man was not around like I had planned. In fact, nothing was going as planned. The roof was falling in on me. My life began to crumble before my very eyes. I kind of understood the whole idea of God being in control, but I always questioned it. That is, if God is in control then why does He allow such failures and disappointments to happen to me? I did believe that God was pointing out my failures so I would understand the truth.

As Christians, we cannot live this life on our own. Even though God did not put me in the situation I found myself in, He allowed me to realize my insufficiencies so I would depend more on Him. Failures help you build a dependence upon God, which strengthens your relationship with Him.

The Spring semester came along and this time I gave myself the pep talk—words of affirmation and positive thinking and all that. I went in with the mindset: "If I just do my best, I will succeed this time." As usual, I had a plan for how things were going to work out. I had a planner both on my phone and on paper, so I knew I was going to be good this time around. This semester labs and clinicals were added to the traditional lectures. That meant that in order to pass the class I had to pass the theory lecture along with the clinical and the lab. Three classes in one. But I had a plan.

The semester started and clinical was a thirteen-hour day. I was pregnant, well into my last trimester. The most tiresome trimester of them all for me. I had to be up by 4:30 am to be ready to hit the road by 5:45 am to make it to clinical by 6:30 am. You can imagine how hard this was for me. But I did it. Every morning I would wake up on time and struggle my way out of the house and I made it on time every single day. I was never late because I was determined. There was no turning back now. This was it for me. I would start each morning with words of affirmation instead of just praying. I was busy telling myself how I was strong, I was smart, and that I could do it.

Words of affirmation are great, and I still use them to this day, but I did not do the most important thing I needed to do: Submit to God and allow Him to be in control. He was my strength, not me. But there I was telling myself each morning how strong I was. The LORD is and has always been, my strength. It took me failing over and over again to realize I was made strong in my weakness because He was my strength. Like He told Paul in 2 Corinthians 12:9, "My strength is made perfect in weakness."

Daily doing all I could and more to succeed, I was still not passing my exams and was always nervous during lab. Here I was again, new semester and I was struggling to pass. I worked on the weekends doing night shift work, which did not really affect my classes. It helped me focus on my classes during the week and enabled me to make extra money on the weekends. I had time to study at work as well, and I used tutors, but I was always a couple of points short of passing on most exams. Week after week my grades were getting worse. They were so bad my professor had a meeting with me to see what was going on in my life. Of course, I played it off as if I was okay because I was a professional at hiding the truth. I was ashamed of telling people what was actually going on in my life. I knew and that was good enough, I did not need anyone else to criticize me. My teacher was concerned and only wanted to see if there was anything she could do to help. She cared about me and she knew I was not stupid. She had confidence in me and wanted to lend a helping hand.

When you are living a life of shame you shy away from telling others your business because you're simply too embarrassed. Then you just get into the habit of pretending everything is okay. As evidenced by my performance in class she knew I was not okay, and that I really needed help. I did not want to allow anyone in my personal space, so I isolated myself even more than usual. I acted as if I was Miss Independent, as if I could do it all by myself. I had gotten myself in the mess I was in and I had a plan to get myself out, not knowing the roof was caving in more and more as each day went by. So, I rejected the help I needed and told my professor I was probably not doing well because of the pregnancy. Mind you, there were many others who were pregnant in my class. In fact, one lady was pregnant with twins.

I kept on failing my exams and my grades were getting lower and lower. I had to continually re-demonstrate my skills in lab class. I was always nervous in the lab and was constantly afraid I would forget everything as soon as I was in the middle of performing a skill. One day at lab I was performing a skill so terribly the instructor noticed it and told me to stop and go into her office with her. She asked me to sit down and just breathe deeply in and out for a couple of minutes before she even said anything. She could tell I was carrying a heavy load and just needed to breathe. I did as she asked and all I felt was cold tears starting to stream down my face. I burst out crying and she just kept saying, "It's okay to cry Saffie. Crying is not a sign of weakness. Cry as long and as loud as you want. I will sit here, and you let me know when you are ready to talk."

I looked at her and just kept crying harder and harder. It was the kind of cry when you just really need to get something out. It felt like I just needed to cry and get it out and she let me do just that. It must have been at least fifteen to twenty minutes of me crying in her office. When I was all done, I felt a sense of relief, like something had come out of my chest. I looked at her and said, "Thank you, I think I just needed to cry, and I am okay now." With my oh-so-big belly in front of me, I thanked her again and walked out. She called to me as I was stepping out and said, "Take care of yourself and the baby. It's okay to not understand it all right now, take it one day at a time." She made that statement as if she had been living in my head. I did not understand what was happening in my life, and I did not try to understand. I just wanted to move past this season of failure and move on to the next season.

Looking back, I have learned each season has its hardships and joys, yes, even joys in the season of failures. During my season of failures, I learned many vital lessons that have shaped me into the woman I am still becoming. And I pray so for you as well, whatever season you may be in right now. Take the time to recognize what season you are in and do not compare yourself with others. I wanted to succeed so badly because I did not want to be left behind. I wanted to graduate with my friend. We were accepted into the program together and I wanted us to graduate together.

Once you acknowledge the season and purpose of the season you are in then you can remain at peace throughout the process. I did not fully understand the season or the purpose of the season until it was over, and sometimes that may be the case with you, too. You may not realize the season or its purpose until you look back. But realizing the season and its purpose will help you to keep pressing forward and not give up. Failures are certainly part of life, there may not be a way to safeguard yourself from failures, but there are ways to steer through them.

As the second semester was coming to an end, once again my grades were not progressing, they were dropping with each exam. However, God continued to strengthen me day after day. I was failing, but I never once thought of quitting. I kept on going to class and studying. Each day I woke up I saw it as an opportunity to succeed. I was always so hopeful; hope kept me going. I remember telling myself, "I know next time I will do better, I will pass the next exam," even though I kept failing. I know it's the legendary cliché to say, "Never give up," but it is entirely true. When you develop deep enough meanings for succeeding, you learn to never ever give up on your goals and dreams, no matter what the situation, no matter the constant failures. You keep pushing day after day, hoping to learn and improve, even if it's just a little. No matter how many times you repeat a class, or how many people are laughing at you, and even if you feel overlooked—never stop working on your dreams. With each failure, you learn something new to take with you to the next level.

I knew I could not stop trying. I wanted to succeed so badly I did not mind failure because I knew in my heart it was just a matter of time. As long as I was repeating the classes, I was guaranteed to pass someday. This hope kept me going,

The semester came to an end and I knew deep within me that I was going to fail again but I remained hopeful that just maybe, somehow, I would pull through and pass. After the final exam, they had us write our phone numbers down on the answer card. Our teachers would call you if you failed. Of course, I knew she was going to call me again, so that day on my way home I turned my phone off, just like I did the previous semester. I did not want to talk about my failure, I just wanted to listen to the voice message. Sure, enough, the time came, and I turned on my phone. I had a new message from a new phone number and my heart was racing. Even though I knew what the message was going to be I was still very nervous to listen to it. The truth hurts, even when we know.

After staring at the phone for a while, I finally listened to the voice message and I heard the professor's voice "I am sorry to inform you, Saffie, that you did not pass NURS 201 this semester." Once I heard it, I hung up the phone without even finishing the entire message. I was so sad. I leaned against the wall and slowly slid down to the floor and rolled on my side and cried myself to sleep. I woke up that afternoon and said to myself, *Well there goes my graduation pushed back another year.* I knew right then I was going to repeat the course and had no choice but to keep trying. Yes, there were times I felt like I had nothing left to give. No matter how hard I kept trying to study I kept hitting roadblocks that would hold me back from succeeding.

Even when you feel like you are defeated, you can overcome obstacles when you keep pushing through the hard times. At one point or another, you will find the drive within yourself to create something worthwhile. One of the classes I failed in nursing school was Psychiatric. This class was different, we learned more therapeutic communication skills; that is, how to talk with patients with mental disorders. I remember having a hard time using the correct terminology and asking open-ended questions. I struggled quite a bit with that class. But when I took that class for the second time, I did learn something.

My professor would always say, "It's okay to make mistakes." She would say leaning and progressing comes from doing something wrong and being taught how to do it right. Once I got that foundation it made sense. I can now say that therapeutic communication is one of my strongest skills as a nurse. Just like riding a bike without training wheels, it is not easy, but once you learn how to do it, it becomes one of life's many skills you will never forget.

I was set to graduate from nursing school in 2013. Well, that was the year I was going to graduate if I was successful in every class as planned. But God had a different plan all along. I ended up graduating two years later. I was disappointed to know I had spent an extra two years to graduate, but I did!

Success does not always come exactly as we planned but the trick is to keep your eyes on the goal and not the situation. It may very well take you an extra year or two, or three or four or ten, but at the end of it all you will come out on top. It's during the failures, disappointments, obstacles, confusion, shame, pain, frustration, lack, and fears that you become strengthened and empowered. Your season of failures, in one sense, is your season of successes as well. You will have learned the hard way, yes, but you will have learned a great deal about yourself, your faith in God, and your life purpose.

During the season of failures, you need to remember it's just a matter of time before you come out on the other side. There is a light at the end of the tunnel, but you will only be able to see the light when you make up your mind to move in its direction. God had it all figured out for you before you were even a thought, before you were created in your mother's womb. You were created for greatness, to be a shining star, to be a light so bright you can supply light to the entire world. "You are the head and not the tail, you are above and not beneath" (Deuteronomy 28:13).

Never look down on yourself because of what you have gone through, someone had to take the bullet for the team. Don't let your light dim, allow it to shine even through your pain. It was all meant to build you and strengthen you. Very often we become so passionate about a thing we can taste success. Remember this, if you fail, it's not the end of the road for you, take it as a new beginning. It's an opportunity to pick yourself up and try again, but with the second or tenth time, you now have the wisdom, knowledge, and experience gleaned from your past failures.

The Girl I Never Knew

Every wise woman buildeth her house: but the foolish plucketh it down with her hands.

Proverbs 14:1

Everyone knows me as nice and pleasant Saffie. I simply adore people; I genuinely see the best in everyone and tell them, especially my man. When I see a smart person, I tell them they are smart, when I see a beautiful girl or boy, I tell them. When I see a sweet person, I tell them. I had respect and love for my man. I know men crave respect and admiration, that's just the way they are wired, just as women are wired to crave love. So I knew how to give my man exactly want he needed and when he needed it.

Until I met the girl I never knew.

It was not until we were married that I discovered another side of me. After my many failures in school, while he was incarcerated, he found Christ and had given his life completely to God. He was my inspiration. I remember every Wednesday when I would go to see him at 2 pm after a very long wait in the waiting area, when he saw me, he always had the biggest smile on his face. He was so happy to see me. He would remind me how much God loves me and how everything happens for a reason. He would tell me how things were going to get better soon. He would spend the first fifteen minutes of our thirty minutes together encouraging me and reminding me of God's love before he would go into his "lovie dovie" stuff. He sincerely loved me and wanted me to be happy despite the difficulties we were facing. He knew I needed to be reminded daily of how much he loved me, and I knew he needed me to respect and admire him daily.

The love he showed me made me confident and the respect I gave him made him a better, more confident man. The more I respected and admired him the more he showed me unconditional love. When you give your man some sweet adoration you will enjoy a great deal of sweet lovin' in return. I adored him unconditionally, even before he was incarcerated; I did not wait until he was nice or affectionate with me. I loved him as he was. You do not have to wait to adore your spouse until he is one-hundred percent adorable. The truth is he may never be at that one-hundred percent mark.

His favorite thing was when I would be specific and say things like, "You are such a strong man, you picked that up with such ease," "Thank you so much for getting me my favorite drink on your way home," "I really appreciate you for helping out with such and such." Noticing what your man does and making it a big deal is how you adore him for what he does. Trust me it works, try it and see what happens.

One thing I did was make sure I adored him physically as well as emotionally and mentally. Yes, I know I was not married to him yet when I was doing those things, but that's why you will do the right thing by waiting until marriage to be a wife and not being a wife while you are still a girlfriend. I adored him physically, I mean let's be honest if you do not adore him in this area who else will, this is one thing the two of you should share together. You do not have to wait until you are intimate to tell him how great he was in the bedroom. Tell him how great he does it at breakfast or lunch or through texting or video chatting or however you communicate throughout the day. These things make a world of difference in building a man's confidence.

Listen to your husband, adore him by listening to him. Men love and need their wife's undivided attention. If you want to become his confidant and learn more about his daily struggles and the areas he needs encouragement in, adore him by listening to him. While still dating I would drop whatever I was doing when he called or wanted me to listen to him. Everything stopped for him and boy did I wish I would have continued this behavior but while I did it, it was almost magical. I gained bonus loving points. Which meant extra loving for me, and we all know all a girl needs is some loving and attention and everything will be good.

Did I also mention he meant the world to me? The entire universe is what he meant to me. You get the idea, I loved him, and he was my rock. While Jesus was supposed to be my rock, I was busy making a human being my rock. Looking back, no wonder I failed at being a wife to him. You need to put your husband first after God. When I used to hear people say, "You put your man first," I took it literally, and I put him first before God. But what that really means is that you should put him first above all other human beings in your life, like your children, family, and friends—he comes first. But remember, if you do not understand or remember anything else in life, always put God, the LORD Almighty first in your life.

Find creative ways to carve out time for your husband because he needs to feel wanted. Do not ever be too busy to spend time with your one and only—that's what you call him anyway, so you might want to live by your words. I know women: We like to run our mouths sometimes, so, while you are running your mouth use some adorable words to let others know what you see in your husband. Yes, a compliment given at home is important but there is something about giving a compliment to your husband in front of others also, this is a magnified thing. Build him up in front of others. Now, I am not saying to overdo. Be careful what you say about your husband in front of other females, a nice compliment or two is great but do not overshare. You are welcome, you will thank me later.

I learned from my mistakes, so I am not a professional at this. I'm just sharing some of the life lessons I have learned in my twenty-seven years of living in this very confused and complicated world. Mistakes bring on lessons that make us better individuals. I got you sister, I went through the confusion alone, but I want to share the benefits of my mistakes and failures with all my sisters, my fellow women.

So right about now, you are probably thinking, *So what was she talking about when she said the girl I never knew?* I am glad you asked. I just wanted to tell you about the girl I knew before you meet the girl I never knew.

The love of my life was finally being released from prison and coming home to his family. I was more excited than ever. Our son was about ten months old at that time. He had never seen his father except in pictures and his father had never seen his son. I was not allowed to take him with me when I went to visit the jail on Wednesdays. I remember that day like it was just yesterday. I couldn't wait to see him, hug him, and have him touch and hold me as a husband again. He was gone for almost two years. Yes, I was faithful, I waited for him the entire time. I'm not sure how I did it, but God helped me through that painful and lonely time. I waited for my man, and he came back to me exactly how he left me.

Love is many things and many different things to different people. For some, it's joy, security, strength, and more. But I came to understand for those in a long-distance relationship, love becomes a wireless network. Our love became a wireless connection through which we communicated. He would call me daily for twenty-seven minutes, that's how long the prison phone allowed us to talk on one phone call. This was a test of our patience, as we kept loving each other daily without any physical contact. We were both eagerly awaiting the day when we would see and hold each other again.

Once his release date was confirmed I got a calendar and began to strike the days off. As the day came closer and closer, I was dying with anticipation. I wanted to look good for him so I went shopping for clothes I knew he would like to see me in. He loved seeing me in nicely fitted clothes, especially pencil skirts and dresses so I did as he would like and dressed in something fitted with my hair done just as I knew he would like it.

He always gave me compliments when I had on a fitted shirt or dress. Again, doing things your husband likes is very important—I had the concept down, but I was doing these things at the wrong time. But I knew what he wanted and did just that. The day came and I was so excited to finally see him after being apart for so long. I went as usual and sat in the waiting area, but this time I was happy and even the people checking me in noticed the excitement and asked if I was there to pick up someone who was being released. I replied and said, "Yes sir, I am here to pick up my man." He laughed and said, "I can tell you are here for a loved one who is being released." Some of the others remembered me from my usual Wednesday visits. The joy I felt that day was so incredibly deep.

Now that he knew God, he kept telling me we were living a life of sin and needed to get married. I thought it was a good idea, but he had been saying he wanted to get married since he was incarcerated, I just thought it was because he was in jail. You know when men are locked up, all of a sudden they want to get married. All they can do is think of a fairy tale life, and how they cannot wait to live the fairy tale after their sentence, so I thought it was jail talk. If you have ever had a loved one in jail you know there is jail talk and then there's real talk. But this was real talk. He had been reading the Bible and kept saying fornication is a sin and since we love each other why not just get married and live a life of obedience to the Word of God.

He came home and told his Dad he wanted to marry me. So, one day we went to the courthouse and made it official. Ta-da, we were married. Nothing really felt different within, I stilled loved him as I had always loved him. For some weird reason, I thought that when you got married it was supposed to feel different. Or maybe it was just me, I couldn't tell if it was supposed to feel different or not considering it was my first time being married. But life went on. I was now a wife and he a husband. I remember being obsessed with the idea of being a wife. I loved talking to strangers in public and saying things like, "My husband and I." "My Husband this, my Husband that," like he did not have a name anymore. It was cool while it lasted. One thing I can say about it is that you do not have to go around constantly talking about your husband to show how much you both are in love—just be natural about it. I sure did my part in flaunting my ring, especially when I saw men looking at me. I made sure they saw my ring, which did nothing for them anyways. Men in the world do not care if you are married, sometimes when I would say, "I am married," they would reply and say, "And so?" They have no respect for marriage.

I was busy showing off and putting my ring in people's faces instead of truly being the wife I could have been. I liked the idea of being a wife, but not so much the responsibilities and duties of a wife. I liked saying I was a wife. Even the way I took pictures changed—my ring became the focal point of my photographs. I can honestly say I was not trying to make anyone jealous, I just liked the idea of having a ring on my finger and telling people I was married. It was a great feeling. Marriage is still one of my favorite things in the world. I love being loved. He was a loving and very affectionate husband to me, and I loved every second of it. He would come home from work and want to eat dinner and cuddle up on the couch and watch a movie together before going to bed.

I started noticing my respect and adoration for him fading away. I was not as respectful as I had been or as adoring as I had been at first. Looking back now, I know exactly what went wrong initially. My behavior toward him changed. This made him very frustrated and he did not know how to confront the matter. We started fighting more and more, even in front of our son. The fighting got more intense each time. He would tell me to do a simple task and I would talk back and say, "No, why don't you do it." I remember saying things, like, "Do I look like your slave? What's wrong with your hands?" And then it went from just having a smart mouth to me being verbally abusive to him, calling him out and belittling him in private and in public. I found myself in this place where I was busy breaking my husband down instead of being the woman who built him up like I had all those years before we were married.

Something went wrong, I became the foolish woman who foolishly tears down her husband and her home. With my mouth, I continued to destroy and devastate what I was supposed to be building. As the months went by, I became worse and worse. I went from using my mouth to using my hands. I started hitting him, I would throw things at him: the remote, books, spoons, a knife, a hot iron, or whatever was handy at the moment. There was this rage inside of me that I knew nothing about. I blew up every time I was angry—I lost control, I became the girl I never knew. I have never been a victim of physical abuse but somehow, I became an abusive wife. He was so fearful for his life when I would get upset that he would just manage to get his car keys and leave. He always ran from me. Sometimes when he ran out, I would run out chasing him and stand in front of the car. He would beg me to please stop and get back in the house.

My little sister saw this day in and day out, she was the only one who knew besides our one-year-old son. I spent more of my time fighting him and chasing him out of the house than anything else. I did not know I had a problem. This behavior continued, and he went from just going for a car ride to cool off to not coming home. But still, I did not care, I had anger building up in my heart and I wanted to hurt him every time I was upset. And it did not take much to get me upset. If he looked at me a certain way, I got upset at him. If he wanted to watch sports instead of watching what I wanted I got upset and had a reason to start the madness. I was tearing my husband and my home down with my bare hands.

One time I was ironing my uniform for school and got so upset that I yelled at him that if he continued whatever it was he was doing I was going to iron his face too. I felt like I was being controlled internally, I was not myself. There was this girl inside me making all these foolish choices to destroy our marriage from within. I became so selfish and was so self-centered, that as far as I was concerned, I was the center of the universe. if I wanted to do something, my feeling at that time was that he had better not say anything about it or against it. I ignored my husband's feelings and interests. I would insist on having things my way and my way only, if they didn't go my way, then a rage-filled wife would be there to punish him. And on top of that, I used my power by withholding sex from him. We all know there is lots of power in that, and oh boy did I abuse it. You know the saying if he's not getting it at home, he'll find a way to get it. All the "please and thank you's" were dead to me. When I wanted something, I demanded it.

To add more fuel to the fire, our son was more important to me than my husband. Never let your children become more important than your spouse. My son did not care if I looked good or attempted to look good when I came home, so I expected my husband to respond the same. I had my mommy hat on always, it was always about the kid. Do not get so consumed in the mommy world that you forget to care for yourself and be sexy for your husband. Before I had my son, one thing I always made sure of was wearing my sexy lingerie to bed. After the baby, I was always in some ugly granny gown, like the ones you wear at the hospital without the strings in the back, just hideous. And then on top of that, I would act like I was his mother. Do not act like you are his mother—you are NOT his mother! I remember saying things like, "I have two children including my husband," and controlling everything he did. Things like telling him to make sure he dressed appropriately for the weather as if he couldn't figure it out on his own. Oh, and my favorite one, I could not wait to say, "I told you," That was the thing he hated the most.

When he made a mistake, I magnified it. However, I always jumped in to save him, so we did not have to suffer the consequences of his mistakes. It is very important to allow your spouse to learn from his mistakes. He does not need his wife to always jump in and fix things. He can only learn if you allow him. I could have outlined everything

I needed him to do down to the smallest details as if he was a toddler who could not figure things out on his own. The thing is this man could do anything and I had no reason to dominate things, but I did.

You are his wife, not his mother. He's got his mother to play that role, and his mother does not need your help in that area, she's got that covered. You married a man, not a toddler, treat him with respect, as you would respect any other adult. Your husband needs a wife, that's why he left his parent's home and joined you to build his own family. No need to say things like, "Make sure you wear a hat today the weather is cold outside," he can figure it out. Just pray he checks the weather before getting dressed so that he wears his hat so he does not get sick. Kiss him goodbye when he leaves and tell him you love him, that's what he needs from you, wifey.

As a young lady, I thought I had my life all figured out. I went into marriage without consulting my Heavenly Father, or my earthly father. The idea of marriage was music to my ears, and it was all I wanted. All I was concerned with was getting married and being married to the man I was madly in love with. A part of me was not ready to get my parents involved in the marriage due to how we met. My parents thought I deserved better. I was thought to be better than to go around getting pregnant by a man who was already in a relationship.

So, because of my fear of telling them the whole truth, I decided to completely leave them out of the equation. Considering what my mother went through with my father and the second wife, I knew she would especially not be in favor of such a marriage. I grew up seeing how much pain my mother endured and now here I was involved in a relationship in which I was the other woman until I became pregnant and the first woman decided to opt-out. In other words, I came in and tore apart a relationship I had no business involving myself in the first place. I played a big part in wrecking their home. Yes, you can call me "the homewrecker." It's okay, that was before I completely surrendered my life to Christ. I am now a new creation in Christ Jesus.

Marriage is supposed to be two families coming together in unity and becoming one. In our situation, it was two young people who had decided to come together as one without consulting God or our parents altogether. My late father-in-law did know, and he was at the courthouse with us that day. He blessed our marriage. But my husband's mother was not aware. And again, we purposely left her out of the equation because she also knew the truth about our relationship. And I will never forget our conversation the day she told me he was in a relationship with a baby on the way. It was nine years later and now here we were getting married, we both knew not to tell her. She is honestly a great woman and wanted the best for both her son and me, but life happens and here we were married.

Because my husband had given his life to Christ while he was incarcerated, I believed it was God's will for me to marry him. Many times, as Christians, we think just because someone is saved and is pursuing us it must be the will of God. I mean he was Christian, and we could finally stop fornicating and live a righteous life. It seemed as if it was the will of God because I knew that he knew God, so God must have confirmed to him that we were meant to be together. Just because someone is saved and knows God does not mean that they are your divinely-chosen husband.

You must first seek the face of God on your own for any decision. Just because something sounds like a great idea does not mean it's from God. It's vital to connect yourself to the Father when making life-changing decisions such as getting married. Marriage is a covenant, that is intended by the LORD to be a lifetime relationship between a man and a woman. Marriage is a vow you make to God, to each other, your families and friends to remain committed, in an unconditional love relationship. In order to remain in this convent, it must first be ordained by God, not you or your spouse. You should wait for confirmation from God. Wait for confirmation from God only before walking down the aisle, or if you are anything like myself, before going into a courtroom and signing a marriage certificate. Save yourself the turmoil and just wait on God. Marriage is a beautiful thing, and you will see and enjoy its beauty when it's with the right person.

It was as if we were both trying to force the wrong puzzle pieces into the big picture. And when you put in the wrong piece you will never be able to put in the correct piece until you realize the mistake and then remove the wrong piece to make room for the correct piece to take its place. You must make room for the correct piece. A piece being wrong does not make it bad, it's just not in the correct place for it to take its shape or fit where it was made to fit. Many puzzle pieces out there are where they are meant to be but are trying to fit in a space either too big or too tight for them. LORD, please help us find our correct space to take shape and get out of the habit of trying to fit into just any space.

You will never feel equipped for a space that was not meant for you to fill. You will never change the shape of the space. Stop wondering why you never seemed to be enough, why you cannot be a great wife to him. Stop wondering and seek God. Change does not take place in one moment, it takes time. God will surely guide you to the right husband. Do not be discouraged, with God all things are possible. And if you are already with the right husband and still do not know how to act—how to treat your king like the king he is— you need to seek the face of God for guidance. He will surely guide you into the ways of being a virtuous wife, whom the heart of her husband safely trusts.

May I refer you to Proverbs 31? Read the entire chapter and you will no doubt gain some biblical wisdom on how to be a virtuous wife. The first time I read it I laughed. I could not relate to her at first, but I hope you do. Allow her to inspire you, or at least be open to learning from her. It may be difficult to understand her if you have never been anything like her, which was the case for me at first. But I can humbly say that I am learning how to first understand her and then learn from her. Give yourself time to warm up to her, especially as a modern-day wife. To all my independent women out there, it's okay to also be a virtuous woman and wife. I do not honestly think there are enough days in one's life to learn how to be exactly like her but allow her to inspire you to be a virtuous woman. Her strength and dignity certainly did not come from her looks or achievements; they are a result of her deep respect for God.

The Virtuous Wife

Who can find a virtuous wife?
For her worth is far above rubies.
The heart of her husband safely trusts her;
So he will have no lack of gain.
She does him good and not evil
All the days of her life.
She seeks wool and flax,
And willingly works with her hands.
She is like the merchant ships,
She brings her food from afar.
She also rises while it is yet night,
And provides food for her household,
And a portion for her maidservants.
She considers a field and buys it;
From her profits she plants a vineyard.
She girds herself with strength,
And strengthens her arms.
She perceives that her merchandise is good,
And her lamp does not go out by night.
She stretches out her hands to the distaff,
And her hand holds the spindle.
She extends her hand to the poor,
Yes, she reaches out her hands to the needy.

The Girl I Never Knew

She is not afraid of snow for her household,
For all her household is clothed with scarlet.
She makes tapestry for herself;
Her clothing is fine linen and purple.
Her husband is known in the gates,
When he sits among the elders of the land.
She makes linen garments and sells them,
And supplies sashes for the merchants.
Strength and honor are her clothing;
She shall rejoice in time to come.
She opens her mouth with wisdom,
And on her tongue is the law of kindness.
She watches over the ways of her household,
And does not eat the bread of idleness.
Her children rise up and call her blessed;
Her husband also, and he praises her:
"Many daughters have done well,
But you excel them all."
Charm is deceitful and beauty is passing,
But a woman who fears the LORD, she shall be praised.
Give her of the fruit of her hands,
And let her own works praise her in the gates.

Proverbs 31:10-31 NKJV

1+1=3

For this cause shall a man leave his father and mother, and shall be joined unto his wife, and they two shall be one flesh.

Ephesians 5:31 NKJV

I know, addition is fundamental, we all learned how to add in elementary school. So then you may question, *Why does one plus one equal three, then?* That was the same question I asked my husband when I found out there was another woman having his baby while we were still married to each other. They say the "two shall become one," not three. But I guess he had forgotten his addition skills learned back in elementary school. He added one plus one and that somehow, in his mind, came out to equal three instead of two.

Marriage is a beautiful thing, and most young girls dream of one day being married and having the most beautiful wedding they can imagine. In fact, most of us plan out our wedding way before we meet the man. We dream about everything from wearing the most beautiful wedding dress, having the perfect ceremony, hosting the most entertaining and fun reception and the most-liked bridal party. You plan the entire process for that one special day to be the most memorable day of your life. We did not have a wedding like the one I had dreamed of all my life, but I was happy with the simple ceremony at the courthouse. Even though it did not live up to my beautiful-princess-wedding dream, I was pleased.

I can honestly say I was happily married to my husband for a couple of months before everything went south. Then my behavior toward him changed drastically. I barely knew who I was, or the woman I had become, at twenty-one years old. The idea of getting married sounded great to me, so I went with it. I made decisions I should have not made at such a young age, but I also learned some vital lessons that will stick with me for the rest of my life. Yes, I made some mistakes, but looking back, those mistakes have helped shape the woman who I am gradually becoming.

I wanted to be loved and treated with respect, but I was giving my husband the very opposite of what I expected from him. Should you still respect people who do not respect you? The right answer is yes; you do not pay evil with evil or an insult for insult but instead, you should repay evil with a blessing. "Not returning evil for evil or reviling for reviling, but on the contrary blessing, knowing that you were called to this, that you may inherit a blessing" (1 Peter 3:9). It's so easy to feel the need to get even with someone who has hurt you. And we see it clearly in my case because of the behavior I displayed to my husband, beating him with just about anything I could lay my hands on. Abusing him verbally and physically forced him to find an escape from me. He started going from driving around the block to cool off to driving off to another woman's arms. And again, this is not an excuse for his actions, but I realize the part my actions played in this situation.

He would drive off the parking lot and not come home until the next day. Because I was so upset and still in my rage, I never even bothered to call him to see where he was. I would pace around the house still cursing and threatening until I got tired and went to bed. This continued for quite a while. He would say or do something to me and "BOOM," I was set on fire and would explode at him, and of course he would just grab his keys and head straight for the door. Month after month this continued. Then he started not coming home for days at a time, to the point where I started noticing his absence. At that point, I would get on the phone and just start screaming and calling him all sorts of names for not coming home and abandoning his family. Since he was now with another woman, he would hang up the phone on me and not answer when I called him back. I would call him so many times in a row until he ultimately just turned off his phone. He was gone. He did not want to talk to me or come home anymore.

So, being the naive twenty-one-year-old that I was, I thought he just wanted space from me since I was being so rude and disrespectful to him. I thought he was just hanging out with his friends. I imagined he was just hanging with his boys and telling them how crazy I had become, not knowing he was with another woman in and day out building something with her. And I found out later that it was not just a fling, either. They were out with it. Everyone knew except me.

Around this time, I had just found out that I was pregnant again with our second child. I was happy because babies are a blessing from God and if I had something to focus on then I would not have time to be crazy, I thought. When I told him I was pregnant, he was happy. But looking back he was acting funny during my entire pregnancy. He became more and more distant from me. He was always in a hurry. Again, I just let him be and continued doing my thing and I didn't worry about it. but I noticed he was losing weight and I remember one day I even mentioned it to him. I said, "You look stressed, and you are losing weight, are you okay?" He looked at me like I was crazy. So, I went about my day. *Oh well, I hope he's ok*, I thought to myself.

I was still attending church regularly, and people started asking about him because he was not around enough to come to church on Sundays or mid-week Bible studies with us like he had been. It is one thing to notice that your spouse is acting a certain way but it's whole other ball game to know that other people around you are also starting to notice. At this point, I become sad and started blaming myself for his actions. I said things like, "Oh, he's not around because I pushed him out with my behavior."

I did the whole blaming myself thing for a long time instead of looking at the problem and getting the help we both needed. In any situation it's crucial to acknowledge the problem first, then accept that you need help. I just did not know the problem so then I could not accept that we both needed help. We continued living in the mess and ignoring the facts. He was obviously having an affair, but I could not see it. Not only was he having an affair, he was not happy within himself. Those were two major red flags I missed.

He was not coming home because he had somewhere else to go, and he was stressed out and losing weight because he was not happy with the outcome of the affair. The girl he was having the affair with was also pregnant, and I had no idea, but the interesting thing was that everyone else knew. Even my family members knew of the girl and the pregnancy. She was very proud of it. She had no problem telling people even though she knew the news would come back to me. She was telling people who knew me that she was pregnant by my husband. No one told me, instead they looked at me as if I knew and was playing dumb. All this was happening while I was carrying our second child.

I walked around town looking like booboo the fool. It was so obvious that when I would come into a room full of people, they would suddenly stop talking and the place would become silent as I walked in. It was weird, I thought, but maybe they just did not want me to hear what they were saying. Again, it was a huge red flag, but I missed it, again. Looking back now I can say it was obvious but while I was living it, I can honestly say I just wasn't aware of it. That's why everyone thought I was playing dumb.

Another lesson learned: Just because it looks obvious does not mean people know. I had no idea what was going on in my home, even though I lived there. Do not judge others based on what you know of them, they may not even know the facts you know about them. I lived in lala land, walking around smiling and excited about our new addition to the family while my world was going upside down. My pregnancy was smooth. I had no issues because the baby was healthy and I was healthy so there was nothing to worry about. As far as I was concerned everything was good, except the fact that my husband did not want to be around me. But in my head, I knew that I had caused it, so I knew he was going to come around; I just needed to give him space, so I thought. Life went on. I went to school during the week and worked on the weekends and he supported our home financially, so it did not bother me if he came home or not. I just wanted to make sure I was passing my classes and moving forward to the next semester so I could finally graduate from the nursing program that had I failed so many times.

One day when I was about eight months pregnant my aunt called me on my way to class; I remember that day like it was yesterday. I had an exam that day and I remember I was driving on the highway, racing to class, going about seventy miles an hour when the call came in. I saw her name and I instantly knew it was not a call I wanted to answer, so I ignored it. There are certain people who call you and you just know it's something serious. I was on my way to take an important exam, which was a very serious matter for me and I did not want anything to distract me or worry me while I was thinking about the exam. I went in and took my test, and thank goodness, I passed. On my way home, I decided to listen to the voice message while I was driving. That was the worst decision ever. Listening to her voice as she uttered the words, I could sense that something was happening to my body. I remember feeling very warm and the more I listened the hotter my body got. I'm not sure what my body was doing, but I got so hot I had to roll my windows down for cool air.

In summary, she said: "That man you call your husband is out there fooling around with another woman who is currently pregnant by him. I know you did not tell me you are pregnant, but I know you are also pregnant and having a boy, but that girl is having a girl. I am tired of looking at this foolish situation and wanted to inform you." She said the girl's name and her social media name, then she told me to go on Instagram and see her pictures. She went on to say that she was sorry to tell me that bad news, but that I deserved to know the truth.

I felt betrayed by the one person I thought loved me, the breaking of trust was so profound. I guess it was because I had invested too much time, hope, and love in us as a couple. Even though I believed it when I listened to the voice message, I just could not make any sense of it. It seemed crazy! I thought we were standing on a foundation of solid rock in our marriage. I had the idea things happen in marriage, but no matter what happens you stay together because things can get messy and out of control, that's just life. What I did not know was we were standing on ice that was gradually melting underneath us.

I looked her up on the Internet, and sure enough, she was pregnant and flaunting it on Instagram. That, for me, was a different kind of pain, it was a numb feeling. By that point in my life, I can say pain was no stranger to me. I knew what pain felt like. In fact, pain had become a part of my life. Sad to say, but it's a fact. I had been hurt, disappointed, I had been burned, but never had anything made me feel as entirely shattered inside as that did. I was walking as a whole human being on the outside but within I was broken, like a shattered vase. *How could I have allowed someone to mean so much to me when he was capable of knowingly choosing to do things he knew would not only hurt me but embarrass me in such a way?* My concept of my own judgment felt unbalanced and wrong, *How could I have allowed this to happen?* Once again, I was blaming myself.

That's how I found out that the man I had loved and who had loved me all those years had done such a thing. I was at a loss for words. As any woman would, I called him and told him I knew about the girl and the pregnancy. He, of course, denied it and claimed he did not know who the girl was or what I was talking about. With my enormous hope and colossal stupidity, I kind of fell for it and hung up the phone. Honestly, I was hoping it wasn't true, so I wanted to believe him. I thought to myself, *Maybe it was all a mistake, maybe my aunt had mistaken him for someone else.*

You know when you find out the truth about a situation and it is so painful you hope it was either a dream or just a big mistake? I wanted it to be a mistake because I knew it wasn't a dream. I had all the information I needed to believe it was true, but still, I doubted.

It's easy to say what you would do if you found out your spouse had cheated but the reality is, we never truly know how we will react to a situation until we are involved in it. Before I found out about the infidelity, I would have said I absolutely wanted to know about it. But when it actually happened to me, I did not want to know anything about it. I even wished my aunt had never told me. It was simply too painful for me to bear.

The normal thing to do when you encounter pain is to want to run or hide from it. Although he denied it, I wanted to ask others and I was hoping they were going to say it's all a lie. I called my close friends and asked them if they knew anything about it and looking back, they all sounded sure of it. I remember one friend told me: "Saffie, there is always SOME truth to a rumor, or else it would not be a rumor at all," and that stuck with me. She was right. It wasn't just a rumor—as a matter of fact—it was all true. After the conversation with my friend, I sat in the car for hours just crying. I felt angry, betrayed, humiliated, sad, and hurt. My cry went from screaming at the top of my lungs to just staring out into space with tears running down my face. I remember saying to myself that it was just so embarrassing. I didn't need him to confirm, I knew it was true.

After crying that afternoon, I had to get ready for work. So I washed my face and put on my make-up and headed out. I worked the night shift then, so I did what I always did and went in and took care of my overnight patient. While I was there, I focused on work and left my feelings and my harsh reality at the door. When my shift was over the next morning, it was amazing how my reality was right at the door waiting for me. Tears began flowing non-stop the second I got back into my car. The flood racing down my cheeks was uncontrollable, to say the least. Driving home, all I could think about was what I was going to do now that I knew the truth. What was I going to do with this information? I was hurt and felt betrayed, but at the same time, I was wondering what I was going to do, what the immediate future would bring. The most natural thing to do would have been to end the relationship, but I couldn't wrap my mind around that.

With the information out for everyone to see, what would be next? It felt like everyone was all looking at me. I wondered if they were thinking the same thing I was thinking. *What is she going to do now?* He not only cheated on me, but a child came out of it. I could hear the questions in my head but could not answer them. When you love someone, you do not stop loving them automatically when they hurt you—as pathetic as that may sound, I did not know what to do. For the next couple of weeks, I was confused. That was when I looked the most like booboo the fool. I was so lost and confused.

After a couple of conversations with friends and family members, I found the courage to ask him to leave the house. He knew I was confused and not sure of what I was doing, but he respected my request anyway and packed his things and walked out the door. Some of my friends and family were happy for me, at least for a moment, until a few weeks later when they saw him back at home. Yes, he came back. I just wanted to forget about the infidelity altogether and put it behind me—behind us—and move past it all. But, the girl was pregnant, and the baby was going to be born soon. That was something I wasn't going to be able to forget or pass through quickly.

Weeks went by and I went into labor and gave birth to our second son. I was happy once again for a safe delivery and a healthy mother and baby. While we were still in the hospital, he kept going outside for "fresh air." I didn't know at the time, but he was going outside to talk with the other girl because she, too, was going into labor. Our children were born three days apart, both born in the same week. My son was born first and then seventy-two hours later his daughter was born.

During that "interesting" time I had a choice to either continue being sad or to focus on my blessings. I did what I had been doing all along: focus on my children. With my husband back home again, I just wanted to concentrate on us and making things better. I just wanted to be a better person to myself, to my children, to others, and most importantly, to my husband. But it was too late to be nice and be a better wife for him, he was too far gone. I'm not saying he didn't love me still, but he was also in love with the other girl; I could just tell. He probably would have denied it if I had asked him, but I knew in my heart it was true.

The girl was convinced she had her man and she was not going to hold anything back. One day I went through his phone when he was asleep. I knew the password for his phone, so I looked at all the text messages between he and his girlfriend. I read them all from start to finish but that did not trigger me like the post I saw on her Instagram page. She had a picture of him, and the caption was, "My better half." When I saw that I immediately slapped him out of his sleep with the phone and told him to pack up and leave. He was so drunk with sleep, he couldn't make sense of what was going on. I jumped off the bed and went straight for his clothes and yanked them out of the closet and went straight downstairs, walked out the door, and threw them into the trash can. I didn't care, I was half-naked, outside yelling and calling out his name at two in the morning. I was furious. I then ran upstairs again and took the rest of his clothes and shoes and threw those out, too. Then I told him to leave and never come back. He begged and begged to stay, but at that point, I had had enough. The Instagram post was the last straw and I wasn't going to take it anymore!

I yelled at him that he had totally embarrassed me with his cheating and having a baby outside our marriage and now this girl was posting pictures of him on her Instagram calling him her "better half." I told him that he should save his stories for the birds. I finally knew then what I needed to know, and I calmed down a bit and said that I needed him to leave in peace. That time I meant it. I was sure I didn't want him around me anymore. I'd had enough of the foolishness. I was willing to let go for good that time. I didn't need anyone else to tell me anything because in that moment it was clear as day.

I needed time to clear my head. It felt like a wound that was not completely healed had been reopened. It felt even more painful than before. I had a new baby, was trying to heal from the betrayal, and now this embarrassment. I caved in, I went into a shell and I did not want to talk to anyone. I stopped going to church and was angry for some time. Never did I think such a thing was going to happen to me at such a tender age. At twenty-three years old, I had endured so much pain there were times when I wanted to literally jump out of my own body. I just wanted the pain to go away.

God has a way of protecting us and our feelings. I felt broken most days but somehow, I was able to continue with life. I was still smiling and laughing with others around me as if nothing had happened. It was all by the grace of the LORD that I was able to continue after such a tragic thing had happened to me. It wasn't a front either, I was not pretending to be happy or okay. The LORD protected my emotions. The LORD is directly involved in protecting you from the embarrassment. You cannot run away from painful experiences but in the moment of your embarrassment, God's disposition toward you is love, forgiveness, and protection. It's very similar to the story of Adam and Eve in the Garden of Eden when they sinned and ate of the fruit from the tree of knowledge of good and evil. God never stopped loving them or protecting them. He will do exactly that for you and me.

I can testify that the LORD clothed me with His love during this time of embarrassment. Even though it felt like my entire life and sense of being was shattered, the LORD rushed to my aid. My Heavenly Father sustained me, "Surely God is my help; the LORD is the one who sustains me" (Psalm 54:4). The LORD not only loves you, He is your protector, helper, and friend. During this time of my life, it looked painful and felt painful, but I had my protector, my helper, and my friend Who was the only one Who truly knew how I felt and stepped in to my aid.

The Trip

But You, O LORD, are a shield for me, My glory and the
One who lifts up my head.

Psalm 3:3 NKJV

During this season, I spent most of my time being angry at God,
almost blaming Him for the pain I was experiencing. In this psalm,
we see David is reminding us, even when everything seems to be
going against us or our circumstances have turned against us, God
never does. He is always there as your shield and the lifter of your
head. Even though I thought I couldn't see or feel Him. looking back,
I can clearly see He had been with me through it all. And this is so for
you as well, the LORD is right there with you through every season.
He does not pick and choose what seasons of your life He wants to be
involved in; He is actively involved in every season of your life.

With my public humiliation, shame, pain, postpartum depression,
and the reality of being a single mother, I became emotionally unstable.
I was lost and confused. There were days when all I wanted to do was
sleep my pain off my mind. At this point, I had lost all sense of who I
was. I was at the lowest point of my life. I woke up with pain and went
to sleep with pain. Most mornings I was mad at myself for waking up;
it felt as if the pain was waiting for me as I woke up each morning. I
spent most nights tossing and turning in bed for hours until I could
finally fall asleep. This was a dark and painful time. I wanted out of my
body. I felt so lost and alone. There were all these mixed emotions—I
felt sad, angry, numb, scared, lonely, and hurt. I was losing control of
myself and did not know how to get help or to help myself.

At this time, I was angry at God again, *Why me LORD? Why
does it hurt so bad? How do I get out of this dark and painful place
I've found myself in? Where are you, Father? You feel so distant from
me.* These were questions I would ask and statements I would say

to myself daily. Do not get me wrong, the LORD had been there for me all along and looking back now, I see His hand there with me through everything. My Father had been with me through it all. But at the moment, it felt as if I was alone. The pain wasn't going to disappear, my life choices had gotten me where I was. I needed relief and I wanted it fast and easy, but it does not work that way. I felt every bit of the pain and misery.

I started drinking for relief. No one knew, I would only buy one bottle at a time, but I would drink the whole bottle in one sitting and get rid of it so there would be no evidence. This was my new way of numbing the pain, and it worked for a while until I started wanting more and more. I knew the more you drink the greater tolerance you develop but for some reason, I was oblivious when it came to myself. I was becoming dependent on it as my pain relief, at least until I fell asleep. It is interesting the habits you pick up when you're in pain. I have never been into alcohol, in fact, I would always say to people, "I do not drink and would NEVER put any sort of alcohol in my mouth." But here I was in my time of desperation.

Alcohol became my friend, the friend who never talked about me behind my back. Alcohol did not judge me, it did not look at me funny, it didn't call me stupid—it simply did what it's supposed to do. It helped me numbed my emotional pain, it helped me to disconnect from myself. One thing for sure, I did not want to connect with myself, being myself was too disturbing.

Before using drinking as a coping mechanism, I used to see people have a few drinks with friends, laughing, smiling and having a great conversation and making fabulous memories, so I wanted that same feeling. But I was drinking alone and not just a few drinks. I was drinking an entire bottle at a time and going to sleep because I hated being awake. Sleeping was the only thing I wanted to do. While I was asleep, I couldn't feel the pain. I suffered in silence; I couldn't connect with anyone around me. I felt as if everyone was pointing fingers at me and wanted me to be this strong, superwoman. I just wanted to be a kid in the arms of my parents. I the parental love that I needed was lacking.

Because my parents were so far away, I didn't want them to know what was going on. I know how much they love me and if they knew I was hurting I knew it would devastate them, so I kept it to myself. But I could tell they knew something was wrong. The natural thing for parents to do is to protect their child and support them when needed. But being miles away from them, I did not want them to feel the disappointment and mistakes I was facing that they could not help me solve. As parents, I know they would've wanted to go out and hurt the person who had hurt me, or even try to bring me a new man who they think would help me heal. But I knew only God could heal me. I needed my parents, don't get me wrong, it would have been great to have them by my side, but more than anything else I needed my Heavenly Father, the one and only comforter of my soul.

In May 2016, the LORD used a sister of mine to call me one day and ask what I thought of going back home for a week. I thought it was a great idea, but I didn't know how It was going to happen since I had the kids. and I was now alone with all the bills to take care of. Where was I going to come up with the money to buy the oh-so-expensive two-way ticket to Sierra Leone and back? Of course, I told her it was a great idea, but I did not tell her I could not afford it. In fact, she did not know much about what was going on in my life at the time. I was ashamed to tell her all the facts. At times, telling others made me sad and for that reason, I kept a lot of my personal life to myself.

We talked and the phone for a good while and then ended our conversation. I didn't think much about our conversation after that day. I went about my life. A couple of days later she called me again and she started discussing the trip and how long I should stay, how I needed to take off time from work and all. As the conversation went on, I started to realize she was serious about me going to Sierra Leone and thought to myself, *This might really happen.* I had hope,

I've always been a person of hope so hope kicked in. About a week or so later she called me very early in the morning to tell me she had bought me the ticket. I was very happy. God knew I needed a break from my current situation and to look at life from a different angle. Right that moment I begin planning how things were going to work out. The boys were going to stay with their father, I was going to put my things in storage and give up the apartment and go to Sierra Leone for a whole month. I could not afford to leave the apartment for an entire month without a paycheck. I got a calendar and began a count down. I could not wait for the day of my departure to arrive.

As the time was approaching, I was getting more and more excited. I could not wait. A couple of days before the day of the trip God blessed me with one of my very good friends coming by with her twin brothers to help me. I was so broke I could not even afford moving supplies, a moving truck rental, or a storage pace. God blessed me again with a friend who offered to lend me her husband's pickup truck. Another friend offered me her basement to store my stuff for as long as I needed. This was the hand of God at work. He wanted me to take this trip, and that's why he provided everything I needed. I had no money at the time. I could have questioned the process, I had been questioning God all my life, but for some reason, I didn't this time. I just knew He was with me and I went with the flow. I suddenly began trusting God again, knowing He was actively involved in my life.

It's difficult to trust God when your life is falling apart, but when I saw He was working things out in my favor it was much easier for me to trust and believe. This might sound silly but sometimes you might find yourself in situations where your faith is tested, and you begin to lose faith in God. I lost faith in God, in fact, I was very angry with Him. I thought He was far from me. But when I say the LORD is never late, please believe it. He was right on time for me. I needed Him more than ever and He showed up at the right time. I did not know how I was going to fund the trip or the move, but He provided every bit of the money and help I needed through people who were around me. God uses the people around us to bless us.

Our Heavenly Father is gracious to put certain people in our lives. As we know, we are all surrounded by people. We are from families, we all have friends, we have neighbors, work associates, church family, strangers we cross paths with on the regular. Some of these people bring us great joy while some may bring only pain, and there are some who bring both joy and pain, that is the nature of close relationships. Some relationships you choose, but others you may be forced into. Whatever the case, no relationship or interaction with others is outside of God's reach. You may question some of the relationships you find yourself in, but remember in all of them, God is at work. He uses people around us to help us. He only uses humans as His vessels to get His work done here on earth, and He used these friends at a time I needed Him the most. Thank you, friends, for allowing God to use you all.

The big day came and off I went to Sierra Leone, my home county. I was not sure what was ahead of me, but one thing was for certain: I wanted to go anywhere other than where I had been for the past couple of years. I didn't tell my parents I was coming home, I wanted to surprise them. Sixteen hours later I was in Sierra Leone. It felt so good to be back home but at the same time, I was in culture shock. I could not believe how much I had forgotten about my country. Things were not as I had imagined them. Right at the airport, I could tell I was in a different land than where I had been all these years.

America is quite different from Sierra Leone. We arrived at night and I was so tired I was tempted to spend the night with my sister. I wanted to sleep and go see my parents in the morning, but she said, "No, you have to go see them tonight." So, we drove to the house and knocked on the gate. In Africa, all houses have tall fences and gates to keep the thieves away at night. It was about 11 pm and I could hear my parents asking, "Who is that? Who's that knocking this hour?" They weren't so happy someone was at their door at such a late hour. My dad opened the door and saw me. He had the classic surprised look on his face, and he immediate picked me up yelling, "You surprised us! We had no idea it was you!" My mother was so happy she hugged me and kissed my face. With all the excitement, the yelling and screaming, we woke up everybody in the house. Everyone came out and was just happy to see me. The house was filled with excitement.

As the days went by, on my thirty-day trip each day we started the day at my sister's house with praise and worship which lead into prayer for minutes and sometimes hours as the Spirit led. My parents are Muslim and going to church is forbidden in their home. We spent a lot of time in the presence of God, not to mention we went to church three days a week. My relationship with God needed revival and this was the best place and time for it. Slowly but surely the Holy Ghost became alive in me again. I was starting to come alive again. I was a dead body walking without even realizing how empty I was until I began to experience the Holy Ghost come alive in me again.

Jesus said that He was going to the Father and He was leaving us with the Holy Spirit, the Spirit of truth. (See John 16.) I needed it and it's amazing how a lost child like I was began to come alive. I not only saw the difference in me, but I felt it, internally. I was slowing healing. Joy began to visit me as the pain was slowly exiting. Sometimes the pain wanted to linger but the more I spend time with God the more I felt joy. This was a great feeling, the feeling of pure joy, a feeling only the Father can give through the Holy Spirit. The Holy Spirit, Spirit of truth was given to us to live inside of those who believe in Jesus Christ to produce God's character in us, in such a way we cannot do in our own ability. The nine fruits of the Spirit in the book of Galatians are built into our lives—love, joy, peace, longsuffering, gentleness, goodness, faith, meekness, and temperance. (See Galatians 5:22-23.) One by one these fruits of the Spirit began to come alive in me. The same Holy Spirit also performs a vital function for non-believers. The Holy Spirit convicts unbelievers' hearts of God's truth concerning sin. (See John 16:8.) The Holy Spirit tugs on sinners' hearts and minds, to repent and turn to God for forgiveness and salvation, a new life. In Jesus Christ, you will find life and purpose, just like I did.

I found purpose in life again. What I thought was just going to be a fun trip turned into a revival of my mind and spirit. I found God again, I had lost touch with Him. Yes, He had never left me, just like he promises to all His children. But I had lost touch with Him, and that is why it felt like He was far away. When I began spending time in His Word and presence, then things took a turn for me spiritually. The pain did not leave immediately but I felt better, I felt the love I had been longing for. The void was being replaced with the precious love of God. I was on this spiritual high, even my skin glowed differently. I felt like the young vibrant lady I was, laughing and cracking jokes, making others around me laugh. I love to laugh, and it felt great to be laughing again.

This was true joy. This was not circumstantial joy, the kind of joy that is determined by the activates around us. This was not the kind of joy I was used to, the rollercoaster ride of life. This was spiritual joy. This kind of joy has nothing to do with our ever-changing emotions or circumstances. This kind of joy is solely based on God. It's just a joy that abides in your heart that knows no matter what happens to you all is well as long as Jesus is in the midst of it. Because my situation was still the same, my husband was still a cheater, the pain was not completely gone, but I knew Jesus was in the midst of it and that gave me peace of mind and I was joyful. Spiritual joy remains constant; it stabilizes above all emotions and circumstances.

As many of us may know and have experienced, living away in another country can change you forever. You will not be the same and you will see things differently. I had been away since I was eleven years old. Going back home for the first time since we migrated to the

United States felt different. I was so happy to be back home to see my parents who I had not seen in years. I thought the trip was just going to be about going back home to see my family who I missed so much, but I came to discover the trip was a life-changing experience for me. I had lost myself in the midst of all that was going on around me and did not know who I had become. Going back home made me realize I was still so young and needed the love and care of my parents, but most importantly, I surrendered to my heavenly Father completely.

Situations and circumstances can cause you to lose hope or faith in God but always know this now and forever: the LORD loves you and He's always near. You can never be too far gone from His presence. As you go through different emotions just know that His love for you is consistent and unconditional. He doesn't love you less because of your anger, loss of hope or faith, or situation or actions. He only wants the best for you and wants you to completely surrender to His will for you. Not just some areas of your life but all areas of your life.

Cleansing Process

Come now, and let us reason together, saith the LORD:
though your sins be as scarlet, they shall be as white as snow;
though they be red like crimson, they shall be as wool.

Isaiah 1:18

Looking at this scripture we are reminded how God can and will cleanse us, even when it looks virtually impossible to us. The stains of our sins are as scarlet as the Israelites', but God will remove sins' stains from every life as He promised to do for the Israelites. God's Word assures us that if we are indeed willing and obedient, through Jesus, He will forgive and remove even our most permanent stains. All He requires of you is to ask. Will you ask him today to make you clean? I did, and He cleansed me just as He promised.

Knowing and serving God wholeheartedly brought me to a realization of my sins and the need to change and become a better me. The more time I spent in the presence of the LORD, the more I saw the need to change my ways. God loves us and wants us to be clean and purified. The presence of God revealed my weaknesses.

Most days, when I am meditating on the Word during my quiet time, I think it's going to be a peaceful time of just praying and reading the Word. Sometimes I even think it's going to be exciting but then something happens, it's like a light bulb goes on and DING! The LORD shows me something in my life that needs improvement. Every time this happens, I have a choice. It always goes like this; *Am I going to obey? Or am I going to disobey and continue reading?* The many times I tried disobeying and not yielding to the word of God, let's just say it didn't end there. One thing I love about the Holy Spirit, He does not give up. He keeps on saying it until I give in. So, you can listen the first time and save yourself time and discomfort, or you can continue to disobey and remain stuck and uncomfortable.

After running and disobeying for a while I finally realized I was doing myself a disservice by not obeying the first time.

If you are anything like me, it takes a couple of times for things to actually stick. I guess you would like such people "stubborn." Yes, I admit, I was a "stubborn child" but look how in due time God arrested me and I had no choice but to yield to the Word of God. Thank you, Father, Son, and Holy Spirit for not giving up on me so easily. You are not the only "stubborn child" out there. The difference is allowing the Word of God to penetrate in your inner life. The Word of God is a supernatural discerning agent of our mixed motives. The Word sorts out and exposes what is of the flesh when you allow it to.

I just want to encourage you, please do not waste time disobeying. The Word is here to give you abundant life. (See John 10:10.) The devil came to steal, kill, and destroy you. Surround yourself with other Christians who will pray with you and for you. I am fortunate to have a supportive church family. My Spiritual Father, who is also the Senior Pastor of my church, has been nothing but supportive during my cleansing process. Deliverance is a process and doesn't take place in one day. It takes time. Be patient and allow God to completely cleanse you. Remember you are dealing with spirits here and you cannot fight them on your own, it takes the power of God through the Holy Spirit to deliver you and set you free. The Bible tells us the fight is not against flesh and blood only but against spiritual wickedness in high places. "For we wrestle not against flesh and blood, but against principalities, against powers, against the rulers of the darkness of this world, against spiritual wickedness in high places" (Ephesian 6:12).

The Word is here to give you and I abundant life. See, the devil came to steal, kill and destroy (John 10:10). Because he knows he cannot physically kill you, he steals from you and `tries to destroy you by self-destruction. That is why you consistently find yourself engaging in behaviors that are self-destructive. Such behavior, if continued can lead to death. So, allow the word to transform you from the inside out. This process is one of the hardest stages to go through as a child of God. It's not quite comfortable either, I can clearly recall how uncomfortable I felt through my what I call "cleansing process". Honestly, somedays i hated it. Knowing my truth was ok at this point but not knowing how I got there in the first place was quite disturbing to me. so , me being me i would go in my closet and cry out to God, not in prayer but in frustration. I could lock myself in my closet and just cry asking God; how did I get here? How do I get out of this? In my frustration I began to cry for help. Most days it went like this; Lord, I know you want me to stop doing these particular things/behaviors, destructive habits but i don't know how to stop these destructive habits on my own. Please help me Father. "just take it away" take the urge way please LORD, If you don't help me I can't help myself. Please deliver me from this behavior. Don't wait until you experience hard and painful lessons before allowing God to get your attention. I know some of these habits are not obvious, only the Holy Spirit can reveal these deepest secrets to us. When He shows you, you can repent and be forgiven forever and ever. Even David, the King God refers to as "A Man after my own heart" (1 Samuel 13:14) asked God to search for sin and point it out (Psalm 139:23-24). King David knew the significance of repentance.

Let's pray this prayer: Lord, convict my heart of any self-destructive behaviors in my life. Let there be nothing hidden. Cleanse me from any secret sins and teach me to be quick to confess when am wrong. Father, help me to continue to obey you in this in Jesus's mighty name, amen. And thank him for encouraging and strengthening your heart to continue doing what he wants you to do. Continue praying prayers of repentance.

The Lord can and will uproot any plant in you not planted by our heavenly Father (Matthew 15:13). Too many of us have fallen and keeps falling because of pride and the inability to first confess our sins and repent. I know these repentance prayers can be annoying, trust me they were very annoying to me but I needed to pray them to be free. I have learned, it is much better to have God shines his light on my sins and expose then than to continue in them and experience the consequences of sin.

Meditate on these scriptures daily during your "cleansing process"
" 3 When I refused to confess my sin, my body wasted away, and I groaned all day long. 4 Day and night your hand of discipline was heavy on me. My strength evaporated like water in the summer heat. 5 Finally, I confessed all my sins to you and stopped trying to hide my guilt. I said to myself, "I will confess my rebellion to the Lord ." And you forgave me! All my guilt is gone" (Psalm 32:3-5)

23 "Search me, O God, and know my heart; test me and know my anxious thoughts. 24 Point out anything in me that offends you, and lead me along the path of everlasting life". (Psalm 139: 23-24)

He's the God who runs in your directions, even when it does not feel like it. Your past, sin, shame, guilt, and pain can't separate you from his love. You are his forever and ever. As his child, fear the Lord. To fear the Lord is to recognize his attributes; Holy, righteous, all-powerful, all-wise, all-knowing, pure, and almighty. When you recognize the Lord for who he is and who you are (sinful, weak, frail and needy), you will fall at his feet humbly. Only then will God show you how to choose his way. So, I encourage you to fall at the Father's feet today for him to direct your path.

Who are those who fear the Lord? He will show them the path they should choose (Psalm 25:12). When we acknowledge God correctly, we gain a clear picture of ourselves.

I had to lose who I had become to find myself in Christ. Lose your life to find it in Christ. I can honestly say, He is still working on me but I am better than I was before Jesus. Remember God and the devil are seeking after souls. God needs people to work through to enlarge His Kingdom here on earth and so does the devil, he also needs people to work through here on earth to enlarge his kingdom. Think of it this way, they both need souls. As much as God loves you and has a plan for you, the choice is still yours to make. Whose team do you choose to be on? If you choose to be on Jesus' team, the salvation prayer is all you need to say and believe in your heart. The prayer of salvation begins with faith. If I may lead you, say this prayer.

Father, I know that I have sinned and now I want to turn away from my sinful nature. Please forgive me and help me to avoid sin. I believe that Jesus Christ came to die for my sins. Jesus, I receive you as my LORD and Savior, to rule and reign in my heart from this day forward. As I say these words with my lips and believe in my heart, I believe that I am saved and renewed in Jesus' name, amen. Thank you, Jesus, for saving me.

WELCOME to the faith. I pray that the Holy Spirit leads you to a Bible-believing church to gown as a Christian. I love you but Jesus loves you more than you can ever imagine.

Become a Vessel unto Honor

If a man therefore purge himself from these, he shall be a vessel unto honour, sanctified, and meet for the master's use, and prepared unto every good work.

2 Timothy 2:21

This is your chapter to write. I have intentionally left ten blank pages for you to start writing your own story, the story many are waiting to read and hear. You have a life-changing story. Write in faith. Just start. You have the blank pages right here right now. It may not be a book, but whatever that assignment is, start writing it down here and become the person you were created to be. Grab a pen and get to it! I believe in you, but most importantly your heavenly Father knows it's in you. He put it in you. So, Become a Vessel unto Honor!!!!

About the Author:

Saffie True Kamara was born in Sierra Leone, West Africa, and migrated to the United States at age eleven with her little sister. She has two lovely boys, Nehemiah and Noah. She lives in the Washington, D.C., Metropolitan Area. Saffie often refers to herself as "a nobody, found in Christ." She is a servant of God whom He is using as a living testimony to encourage and to lead people to Christ. She is a Registered Nurse by trade.

Saffie's goal is to lead people to Jesus, the Savior of the world. She also strives to encourage people to become a vessel unto honor, fit for the Master's use (See 2 Timothy 2:21). Saffie believes despite your past, family, or cultural background you can still rise and become what God has called you to be. She believes that there's not a life too messed up or too dirty that God cannot clean up and purify for His glory.

CPSIA information can be obtained
at www.ICGtesting.com
Printed in the USA
LVHW032058230320
650904LV00006B/910

9 781640 889651